SPOUSE ABUSE

Assessing & Treating Battered Women, Batterers, & Their Children

Michele Harway, PhD
Marsali Hansen, PhD

Professional Resource Press
Sarasota, Florida

Published by
Professional Resource Press
(An imprint of the Professional Resource Exchange, Inc.)
Post Office Box 15560
Sarasota, FL 34277-1560

Printed in the United States of America

The copy editor for this book was Patricia Hammond, the managing editor was Debra Fink, the production coordinator was Laurie Girsch, and Jami's Graphic Design created the cover.

Library of Congress Cataloging-in-Publication Data

Harway, Michele.
  Spouse abuse : assessing and treating battered women, batterers, and their children / Michele Harway, Marsali Hansen.
        p.   cm.
  Includes bibliographical references and index.
  ISBN 1-56887-005-1
  1. Wife abuse. 2. Abusive men--Rehabilitation. 3. Abused wives--Rehabilitation. 4. Children of abused wives--Rehabilitation.
  I. Hansen, Marsali. II. Title.
  RC569.5.F3H37 1994
  616.85'822--dc20   94-29476
                                                                              CIP

Acknowledgments

We would like to thank the individuals who were instrumental in our completion of this manuscript. These include: Jordan Golan and Michael Meit (at Indiana University of Pennsylvania) and Sally Peace and other staff members, especially the library staff (at the California Family Study Center).

Lenore Walker, EdD, also deserves special mention for allowing us to include her expanded listing of Post-Traumatic Stress Disorder criteria.

Our special thanks and appreciation to our wonderful gentle partners: Bruce E. Antman and Ronald Smith.

Table of Contents

SPOUSE ABUSE

Assessing &
Treating
Battered Women,
Batterers,
& Their Children

1

What Kinds of
Families Are Violent?

HOW COMMON
IS DOMESTIC VIOLENCE?

"The American family and the American home are perhaps as or more violent than any other single American institution or setting. . . . Americans run the greatest risks of assault, physical injury, and even murder in their own homes by members of their own families" (Straus, Gelles, & Steinmetz, 1980, p. 4). Shocking as it may be, this statement tells us something about the prevalence of familial violence in our society.

We present these findings here to convince our readers of the necessity of learning about how to treat spousal abuse and each person affected by it. No longer can clinicians assume that only specialists in domestic violence must be knowledgeable about this problem. In fact, it is highly likely that all practitioners will at some point be treating either a violent individual, the target of that violence, or a child who views the violence. Every clinician, therefore, must be an expert in spousal abuse assessment and treatment. It is our intention, with this book, to provide the information necessary to sensitize clinicians to the issue and to outline treatment strategies and interventions.

It is difficult for clinicians with no personal experience of spousal abuse to understand its insidiousness. "Case Example 1" (pp. 9-10) presents a family in which spousal violence follows a typical course.

Statistics about prevalence of spousal abuse differ for a variety of methodological reasons, such as how violence is defined or measured, who is surveyed, and the context of the study (e.g., when spousal abuse is assessed as part of a study of crime, prevalence statistics are somewhat lower because most do not think of domestic violence as a crime, even though it is). Some of the commonly reported figures are those of Gelles and Straus (1989) which indicate that 1 out of every 6 wives reports that she has been hit by her husband at some point in her marriage. In 6 cases out of 1,000 the attack takes the form of a severe beating, and in 2 cases out of 1,000 the attack involves the use of guns or knives.

Estimates were made that 8.7 million couples experienced at least one assault during 1985 (Straus & Gelles, 1988). The same researchers estimate that in 3.4 million households, the violence had a relatively high risk of causing injury. However, it is said that less than 1 out of every 250 spouse assaults is reported (Steinmetz, 1977), therefore, the statistics are likely to be considerably higher even than those listed above.*

Of course, domestic violence is not restricted to couples who are legally married. Koss (1990) indicates that the proportion of violence in dating relationships is extremely high—fully 50% of couples have experienced it. Likewise, violence is not something unique to heterosexual couples: Renzetti (1993) found that as many as 59% of lesbian couples have also experienced violence. Spousal violence is found in all groups regardless of socioeconomic status, religion, or racial/ethnic background.

These statistics clearly indicate that domestic violence is a problem which affects people from a wide variety of backgrounds.

---

*Because 95% of batterers are men and most of the battered are women (Connors & Harway, 1994), the male pronoun will be used throughout this book to refer to batterers and the female pronoun will refer to those battered.

HOW SERIOUS IS DOMESTIC VIOLENCE?

Some practitioners, aware of the incidence of violence today, are not aware of the seriousness of violent episodes and thus tend to underestimate the danger their clients may experience.

Yet, the research indicates that conjugal assaults tend to have more serious consequences than other types of assaults. The National Crime Survey, while finding conjugal assaults to include only 5% of total reported assaults, indicated that they accounted for 12% of assaults ending in serious injury, 16% of assaults requiring medical care, and 18% of assaults requiring victims to miss at least 1 day's work (Gaquin, 1977-1978).

A study of 300 shelter residents indicates that these women had endured an average of 59 assaults each. Prior to intake, each woman had on the average experienced over five assaults every 4 weeks, for an annualized frequency rate of over 65 conjugal assaults per year. Over 20% stated that they were being assaulted twice or more per week. Sixty-two percent of women who had ever been pregnant during their abusive relationships had been assaulted during a pregnancy. Two-thirds of the sample had experienced at least one assault where they were extensively beaten up or worse. One in 6 had been threatened with a knife or gun by her partner, and one in 30 had actually been attacked with a knife or gun (Okun, 1986). These 300 women reported on intake 28 fractures (most commonly of the nose or jaw) and 22 serious injuries not involving fractures (chronic back injuries, torn ligaments, dislocations, ruptured eardrums, broken teeth, lacerations, stab wounds, bullet wounds). These injuries included only those that had been sustained at the time of intake, not previous injuries.

A frightening finding is that of this group, only 24% of women had ever received medical treatment for injuries sustained during conjugal assaults. The remainder had wanted medical treatment but were prevented by their partner from obtaining it. Sixty-nine percent of these women had experienced at least one assault that resulted in police intervention, and over 17% had received multiple visits from the police.

Unfortunately, the physical effects of spousal abuse are not limited to injuries. In many cases, domestic violence results in murder, with lethality in cases of wife battering most likely to occur when the woman tries to leave (Browne, 1987).

That women are in particular danger is substantiated by the finding that 70% to 80% of women who are murdered are killed by their husband, a member of the family, or a close male friend (cited in R.E. Dobash & R.P. Dobash, 1977-1978).

Thus, serious injury (or death) as a result of domestic violence is highly likely.

CONTEXT WITHIN WHICH
BATTERING OCCURS

Understanding spousal abuse requires an understanding of the cultural context within which battering occurs. "Men who assault their wives are actually living up to cultural prescriptions that are cherished in Western society—aggressiveness, male dominance and female subordination—and they are using physical force as a means to enforce that dominance" (R.E. Dobash & R.P. Dobash, 1979, p. 24).

Sex-role stereotypes may maintain battering as the societal problem that it is today. In fact, a number of researchers, studying the causal pathways for a variety of types of violence, attribute violence to gender-role conflict and hypermasculinity (Connors & Harway, 1994; Lisak & Roth, 1988; O'Neil & Egan, 1993; Pryor, 1992). Another factor is that the traditional family is a system where the balance of power is inherently unequal, mimicking other relationships of men and women, where men have usually held the power and women have been subservient to those in power over them. One of the effects of power imbalance is that women, as the less powerful member of the family, learn to be more accommodating and also to tune in more to the needs of their spouse. This pattern of behavior is accentuated among battered women (as evidenced by the complacency that many battered women exhibit, their difficulties in leaving, and the tendency to placate the batterer so as to avoid repetition of violent episodes). Other research substantiates that females are more emotionally expressive than males. Thus women are seen as being emotional (equated with irrationality), men as nonexpressive (equated with rationality). At the same time, expressions of aggressiveness (which is more characteristic of males) are not typically labelled as expressions of emotion nor as irrational acts.

Expressions of aggression by a batterer toward his wife (even those stemming from a loss of control) fail to be condemned by society because they are role congruent, while fighting back (usually in self-defense) by the wife would be condemned because it is incongruent with the female gender-role.

WHO SEEKS TREATMENT?

We have argued that the statistics cited previously suggest that at some point in their practice all therapists will find in their waiting room either a battered woman, a batterer, the children of these couples, or someone else affected by spousal violence. Thus, it is important to know exactly how these individuals will present when they seek treatment.

Will they come for therapy to rid themselves of the violence? Some recent research suggests otherwise. Holtzworth-Munroe et al. (1992) describe their efforts to find a nonviolent control group for a study of spousal violence. In five different studies, they sought nonviolent maritally distressed couples from psychological and family therapy clinics and nonviolent nondistressed couples from the surrounding community. Among the maritally distressed but allegedly nonviolent couples, 55% to 56% of the men actually reported having at some time engaged in violent behavior toward their wives. Among the nondistressed couples, 30% to 34% of the men (depending on the sample) were violent toward their wives.

In the same study, the percent of husbands who had been violent toward their wives in the previous year ranged from 43% to 46% (depending on the sample) among the distressed couples and 15% to 21% among the nondistressed couples. Although the majority of the violent behaviors were not classified as severe (but did include pushing, grabbing, shoving, throwing things, and slapping), husbands had generally engaged in several different violent behaviors and/or in one violent behavior more than once. Some husbands had engaged in severe violent behaviors such as choking or using a knife or gun.

The Holtzworth-Munroe et al. (1992) study suggests that a critical skill for clinicians, therefore, must be assessment for spousal abuse. In Chapter 3, we will describe how this assessment should be conducted.

One final note: Our interest in this area was motivated by some research we conducted (Hansen, Harway, & Cervantes, 1991; Harway & Hansen, 1993a, 1993b) suggesting that even experienced therapists were not knowledgeable in assessing or treating spousal violence. In both studies, therapists received a mail questionnaire which mentioned a case vignette (of an actual violent family). In the first study, therapists were members of the American Association of Marriage and Family Therapy (AAMFT) and included both master's and doctoral level clinicians representing themselves as marriage counselors, clinical social workers, psychologists, and psychiatrists. After the presentation of the vignette, they were asked to describe what was happening in the family, what interventions they would make, what outcome they would expect from their intervention, and what legal and ethical issues the case raises. When asked to describe what was going on in this case, 40% of practitioners in this sample failed to address the issue of violence (even though the violence was clear in the case). Moreover, among those identifying the conflict, the severity was minimized: Ninety-one percent of those who addressed the conflict considered it mild or moderate.

Recognition of family violence is an important first step, but no less important are the therapists' descriptions of how they would intervene. Because even those who addressed the violence underplayed its seriousness, the interventions they subsequently recommended were inappropriate. Fully 55% of respondents *would not* intervene as if the violence required any immediate action. The results were consistent across characteristics of the respondent (master's or doctoral education, psychologist or other license, and gender). There were few differences by theoretical orientation of the respondent.

The second study also involved a mail questionnaire, this time sent to a random sample of the memberships of several practice divisions of the American Psychological Association (APA; Divisions 12, 29, and 42). A case in which rather extreme domestic violence was implicated was presented to respondents.

Results of the second study support those of Study 1 in that some substantial proportion of our psychologist respondents did not generate appropriate interventions even when told outright that the case was one of domestic violence with a lethal outcome.

The fact that relatively consistent findings were obtained from both studies suggests that many psychotherapists (with a variety of types of training) are unable to formulate appropriate intervention plans even when explicitly told that a case is a violent one. Moreover, it also appears that therapists are unprepared to assess for dangerousness in violent families.

In the second study, diagnoses given by respondents prior to knowing about the homicide were compared to assessments of dynamics made after being told that the case had resulted in a murder. Diagnoses and assessments were remarkably similar: A substantial proportion of respondents used as a diagnosis a V code for marital problems (V61.10 in *DSM-III-R* which corresponds to V61.1 in *DSM-IV*). After being told that a murder had occurred, most still speculated that the underlying dynamics of the case were heavily dependent on the couple's issues. Only a handful of respondents, either before learning of the homicide or after, focused on the pathology of the perpetrator! Moreover, fully one-half of our sample, asked what intervention they could have made prior to the fatal outcome, failed to consider obtaining protection for the wife or of insuring her safety.

WORKING WITH VIOLENT FAMILIES

The data presented in this section make it clear that working with violent families is difficult work, fraught with peril both for the clients and the therapist. Because of the prevalence of spousal abuse and the danger that clients are in, mental health professionals are cautioned to be knowledgeable about this issue, competent in assessment and treatment of violent families, and willing to consider the possibility of abuse even when the clients present with problems seemingly unrelated to violence.

CASE EXAMPLE 1:

Susan and George*

Susan Spence met George Gambrills at a church social. From the first, she was quite taken by him: tall, good-looking, very personable, gainfully employed as an engineer at an aircraft manufacturer, and he had all of the characteristics of a potential marriage partner. George perceived Susan as the woman of his dreams: intelligent, moral, financially able to contribute to a family, and very beautiful. They dated for 8 months. Their courtship was idyllic: George was very romantic; he frequently bought her roses and gifts and took her to expensive restaurants. He enjoyed being with her so much that they spent virtually all of their time together. Susan began to distance herself somewhat from her girlfriends. For one, she had little time left after work that was not spent with George. Also, George had reasons for not liking each of her friends and she began to feel alienated from the individuals themselves. George found himself suspicious of Susan's friends. He felt she should need him and come to him instead, claiming that was what a relationship was supposed to be. By the time he proposed, George was her best and only friend. Susan immediately said yes and began preparing for the wedding. George was intricately involved in the planning. He wanted a fancy white-tie wedding. He wanted a Saturday night wedding at a big hotel in town. He wanted beef Wellington for the main course. He wanted his brother Fred to be best man and his sister Erica to be maid of honor. He said he felt uncomfortable with Susan's brother Tom and did not want him to be an attendant. He wanted his cousins Samantha and Benjamin to be attendants. Susan had dreamed of her wedding for many years. George's plans were very different from the wedding she had envisioned. Though Susan was upset, she was so in love that she acquiesced to all of his requests.

Shortly after the wedding, George seemed to change and began to be abusive. At first he simply put her down. She wasn't as perfect as he thought she was, but then she had never been married before, and with a little instruction. . . . His criticisms increased to nagging and deriding her, expressing unfounded jealousy and spewing insults about her family and work mates. Then he began insisting she restrict her

---

*Names and all identifying characteristics of persons in all case examples have been disguised thoroughly to protect privacy. None of these materials represent any specific client and all materials are composites drawn from numerous cases.

activities, forbidding her to leave the house during her time off, controlling the family finances, and eventually complaining so much about her work that she quit her job. Susan felt relief at quitting her job, as shortly thereafter she discovered she was pregnant. Relationships with her family began to deteriorate since George began to tell her things that relatives had allegedly said about her behind her back. Susan was upset when George forbade her mother staying with her when her baby, George, Jr., was born. However, she thought George would be kinder now that he had the son he had always wanted. Instead, George, Sr., found fault with everything she did for the child. In addition, he did not help with the care of the baby, but would hold him and tell him how inept his mother was. George felt Susan let herself go physically after the birth of the baby and was angry that she no longer looked like the woman he married.

The first time that George struck her, Susan was stunned. He had been yelling at her about her slovenly housekeeping and how poorly she was caring for the child when suddenly he pushed her so hard she fell over the coffee table. He also punched her so hard in the face that her ponytails came undone. The morning following the fight, George was contrite, telling her that he had so much pressure at work that he had lost his mind. He apologized and bought her an exquisite bracelet to make up for hurting her. He promised that it would never happen again.

Unfortunately, the violence continued and became more and more acute and more and more frequent, each time followed by a period of contriteness with George going out of his way to be especially loving to atone for his loss of control. Most of the time, George would slam Susan against the wall, once even going so far as to slam her so severely that her hearing was affected. At other times, George would become enraged and lock her in the apartment, leaving her isolated for days at a time. Young George, Jr., was watching his father. Even at the age of 2 he would copy his father's phrases and put Susan down. Throughout it all, Susan continued to love George, excusing his violence by pointing to the extreme stress of his job and indicating that the real George was the loving man who bought her gifts and acted so lovingly following a fight. She also felt her young son was only going through a "stage" and would learn to behave better.

Susan became pregnant with Catie when George, Jr., was 4. Her husband was angry and complained that they did not have the money for another child. He did not accompany her to the hospital for the birth of their daughter. When Catie was a baby her father refused to have anything to do with her. He began to belittle her just like he belittled Susan. When Catie was 4 she began to complain of headaches. Her pediatrician recognized these as stress related and recommended the family seek counseling.

2

How Much Do You Know About Partner Abuse?

Before continuing with other chapters, readers may want to complete this self-quiz to assess their current knowledge about spousal abuse. The first section of this chapter begins with the self-quiz, continues with answers to the quiz, and concludes with detailed information relating to each correct answer. The self-quiz is an important adjunct to training in this area, since our research (Hansen, Harway, & Cervantes, 1991; Harway & Hansen, 1993a, 1993b) indicates that clinicians feel ill-equipped to intervene with this population. It is likely that the many myths about spousal violence have been accepted as truth by psychotherapists as well as others. The self-quiz was developed for this book based in part on myths about domestic violence in Lenore Walker's (1979) book *The Battered Woman* and in the New Jersey Domestic Violence Model Curriculum.

Self-Quiz

Indicate whether each statement is True (T) or False (F):

_____ 1. Battered women represent only a small percentage of the population.

_____ 2. A person who verbally intimidates or harasses his partner is *not* likely to lash out physically.

_____ 3. Research indicates that battered women are masochistic.

_____ 4. Violence in the home rarely results in *serious* injuries or permanent damage.

_____ 5. Unlike poorer women, middle-class women are not likely to get battered.

_____ 6. Twenty percent of all Americans approve of hitting a spouse on appropriate occasions.

_____ 7. Minority women are battered more frequently than Anglo women.

_____ 8. Women who repeatedly leave and return to violent partners do so *mainly* because they are emotionally unable to separate from them.

_____ 9. Religious beliefs strongly decrease the probability of becoming a batterer.

_____ 10. If spouse abuse is suspected, mental health professionals are required by law to report it to the authorities.

_____ 11. Battered women are uneducated and have few job skills.

_____ 12. Alcohol causes battering when the man drinks.

_____ 13. Batterers are violent in all their relationships.

_____ 14. Batterers are unsuccessful and lack resources to cope with the world.

_____ 15.   The most important goal in working with a battered woman is to help her leave the abusive partner.

_____ 16.   Battering is the single major cause of injuries to women, more than stranger rapes, muggings, and automobile accidents combined.

_____ 17.   Batterers have psychopathic personalities.

_____ 18.   In most parts of the country, police have been unsuccessful in protecting a battered woman.

_____ 19.   It would be appropriate to think of a battered woman as a hostage in her own home.

_____ 20.   A woman's nagging is a major cause of violence in the home.

_____ 21.   The batterer is not a loving partner.

_____ 22.   A wife batterer also beats his children.

_____ 23.   Pregnant women tend to be "immune" to assaults by their partners during the course of their pregnancies.

_____ 24.   Once a battered woman, always a battered woman.

_____ 25.   Once a batterer, always a batterer.

_____ 26.   Threats to turn in a woman to immigration, welfare, or other authorities are considered domestic violence, in that they represent the batterer's efforts to control his partner.

_____ 27.   Some women deserve to be beaten.

_____ 28.   The diagnostic clue "accident prone" may appear in the history of some women.

_____ 29.   Battered women can always leave home.

_____ 30.   Batterers will cease their violence once the couple gets married.

_____ 31. In a battering relationship, often the batterer spontaneously stops being violent permanently, if he is happier.

_____ 32. Children need their father even if he is violent.

_____ 33. It is relatively easy to assess by her personality type whether a woman is likely to be in a battering relationship.

_____ 34. When a woman leaves an abusive relationship, the likelihood of serious injury increases.

_____ 35. The majority of battered women have been hit 1 to 3 times by their partner before being successfully helped.

_____ 36. Though unintentional, many battered women do things that cause their husbands to hit them.

_____ 37. Signs that a partner will become a batterer are usually present during the first few weeks of the relationship.

_____ 38. Upon hearing that a woman is in an abusive relationship, the majority of mental health professionals are most concerned about the woman's safety.

_____ 39. The majority of abused senior citizens are beaten by their partners.

_____ 40. Battering usually occurs when the husband's feelings of love for his partner are replaced by anger and hate.

Self-Quiz Answers

Let us see how you did:

_F_   1.   Battered women represent only a small percentage of the population.

_F_   2.   A person who verbally intimidates or harasses his partner is *not* likely to lash out physically.

_F_   3.   Research indicates that battered women are masochistic.

_F_   4.   Violence in the home rarely results in *serious* injuries or permanent damage.

_F_   5.   Unlike poorer women, middle-class women are not likely to get battered.

_T_   6.   Twenty percent of all Americans approve of hitting a spouse on appropriate occasions.

_F_   7.   Minority women are battered more frequently than Anglo women.

_F_   8.   Women who repeatedly leave and return to violent partners do so *mainly* because they are emotionally unable to separate from them.

_F_   9.   Religious beliefs strongly decrease the probability of becoming a batterer.

_F_   10.   If spouse abuse is suspected, mental health professionals are required by law to report it to the authorities.

_F_   11.   Battered women are uneducated and have few job skills.

_F_   12.   Alcohol causes battering when the man drinks.

_T/F_   13.   Batterers are violent in all their relationships.

_F_   14.   Batterers are unsuccessful and lack resources to cope with the world.

F   15.   The most important goal in working with a battered woman is to help her leave the abusive partner.

T   16.   Battering is the single major cause of injuries to women, more than stranger rapes, muggings, and automobile accidents combined.

F   17.   Batterers have psychopathic personalities.

T   18.   In most parts of the country, police have been unsuccessful in protecting a battered woman.

T   19.   It would be appropriate to think of a battered woman as a hostage in her own home.

F   20.   A woman's nagging is a major cause of violence in the home.

F   21.   The batterer is not a loving partner.

T/F 22.   A wife batterer also beats his children.

F   23.   Pregnant women tend to be "immune" to assaults by their partners during the course of their pregnancies.

F   24.   Once a battered woman, always a battered woman.

T   25.   Once a batterer, always a batterer.

T   26.   Threats to turn in a woman to immigration, welfare, or other authorities are considered domestic violence, in that they represent the batterer's efforts to control his partner.

F   27.   Some women deserve to be beaten.

T   28.   The diagnostic clue "accident prone" may appear in the history of some women.

F   29.   Battered women can always leave home.

F   30.   Batterers will cease their violence once the couple gets married.

__F__ 31. In a battering relationship, often the batterer spontaneously stops being violent permanently, if he is happier.

__F__ 32. Children need their father even if he is violent.

__F__ 33. It is relatively easy to assess by her personality type whether a woman is likely to be in a battering relationship.

__T__ 34. When a woman leaves an abusive relationship, the likelihood of serious injury increases.

__F__ 35. The majority of battered women have been hit 1 to 3 times by their partner before being successfully helped.

__F__ 36. Though unintentional, many battered women do things that cause their husbands to hit them.

__F__ 37. Signs that a partner will become a batterer are usually present during the first few weeks of the relationship.

__F__ 38. Upon hearing that a woman is in an abusive relationship, the majority of mental health professionals are most concerned about the woman's safety.

__T__ 39. The majority of abused senior citizens are beaten by their partners.

__F__ 40. Battering usually occurs when the husband's feelings of love for his partner are replaced by anger and hate.

Detailed Answers

Now for a detailed explanation of the answers on the self-quiz. These detailed answers are organized by topic rather than chronologically. Thus, those statements which refer to general issues regarding physical or psychological violence are presented in the first section. Items relating to the prevalence and seriousness of spousal abuse follow. Myths about violence are followed by cultural issues about battering and the dynamics of battering. The chapter concludes with a discussion about assessment and treatment issues and legal and ethical concerns.

PHYSICAL OR PSYCHOLOGICAL VIOLENCE

Statement 2: *A person who verbally intimidates or harasses his partner is NOT likely to lash out physically.*

This statement is FALSE. Experts on battering agree that physical violence is at one end of the spectrum but that verbal intimidation, harassment, and similar actions represent escalating attempts to control the partner (Walker, 1979). Ultimately these behaviors will lead to physical violence.

Statement 19: *It would be appropriate to think of a battered woman as a hostage in her own home.*

Statement 26: *Threats to turn in a woman to immigration, welfare, or other authorities are considered domestic violence, in that they represent the batterer's efforts to control his partner.*

These statements are TRUE. The escalating violence and control exerted by a batterer includes social isolation of the victim and the severing of her ties with friends and family as a way to get her under his control (Walker, 1984). Eventually, the woman may very much be a hostage in her own home, powerless to leave and frightened for her survival. Threats to turn her in to the authorities also represent ways that the batterer exerts his control over his woman.

PREVALENCE AND SERIOUSNESS

Statement 1:   *Battered women represent only a small percentage of the population.*

This statement is FALSE. Depending on which statistic you consult (and they vary based on definitions of battering and samples selected), anywhere from 3.8 million to 8.7 million couples experience violence. Koss (1990) indicates that 28% to 33% of married couples experience violence at some point during their relationship. Dating violence is also quite common; Koss indicates that as many as 50% of dating couples experience violence. And battering is not restricted to heterosexual couples: Renzetti (1993) reports that as many as 59% of lesbians are in battering relationships. Regardless of which figure you decide to heed, battering affects a substantial proportion of the population.

Statement 4:   *Violence in the home rarely results in SERIOUS injuries or permanent damage.*

This statement is FALSE too (Okun, 1986).

Statement 16:   *Battering is the single major cause of injuries to women, more than stranger rapes, muggings, and automobile accidents combined.*

This statement is TRUE. In addition, battering can be lethal, as 70% to 80% of all women who are killed are murdered by their husband or male partner (cited in R.E. Dobash & R.P. Dobash, 1977-1978). For this reason, any report of violence in the home must always be taken very seriously by the clinician.

MYTHS ABOUT VIOLENCE

Statement 3:   *Research indicates that battered women are masochistic.*

Statement 33: *It is relatively easy to assess by her personality type whether a woman is likely to be in a battering relationship.*

These statements are FALSE. In spite of repeated attempts to profile the predisposing factors to becoming a battered woman, no single profile has been described in the research literature. In fact, Hotaling and Sugarman (1986), examining 400 studies of battering, find that the only common trait shared by women who are battered is a slightly greater tendency than nonbattered women to come from abusive families. Nor has a single study indicated that battered women are likely to be any more masochistic than other women, or to share any other personality constellation with other battered women. In fact, Follingstad, Neckerman, and Vormbrock (1988) have indicated that the symptoms that battered women present in therapy are almost certain to be the *result* of years of battering rather than to provide a causal explanation as to who will be battered.

Statement 8:   *Women who repeatedly leave and return to violent partners do so MAINLY because they are emotionally unable to separate from them.*

Statement 29: *Battered women can always leave home.*

These statements are FALSE. Statistics indicate that battered women leave their batterers more frequently than has been believed. Browne (1987) indicates that battered women make an average of seven attempts to leave before they are able to do so permanently. When these women return, they almost invariably indicate that the person they went to did not take them seriously. Family members have often pushed the women to try harder. Clergy, doctors, and even psychotherapists have often urged battered women to modify their own behavior in order to effect a change in the relationship. Other times, helpers have seemingly been unaware of the physical danger the women are in. Goodstein and Page (1981), for instance, indicate that battered women who presented to a medical emergency setting report having gone to a therapist, usually for only one session, and did not return because the therapist *never even asked them about the battering*. Thus, when a battered woman leaves her batterer and seeks help from another, inability to obtain emotional support is the most common reason for returning to the abusive situation. Other reasons include lack of financial resources and fear for the safety of the children.

Statement 20: *A woman's nagging is a major cause of violence in the home.*

Statement 27: *Some women deserve to be beaten.*

Statement 36: *Though unintentional, many battered women do things that cause their husbands to hit them.*

All of these statements are FALSE. Violence is always the responsibility of the person who commits it. Although nagging can be unpleasant, and battered women may engage in behaviors that are very disagreeable, a batterer has numerous other alternatives to violence, such as leaving the room.

Statement 23: Pregnant women tend to be "immune" to assaults by their partners during the course of their pregnancies.

This statement is FALSE. Pregnant women who have been battered are at high risk during their pregnancy. For some women, the first incidence of battering may in fact have occurred during their pregnancy. Half of all battered women are abused during their pregnancy (Okun, 1986). The breasts, abdomen, and genitals seem to receive the greatest share of the blows. Researchers describe the high incidence of battering during pregnancy as being the result of the batterer's frustration that someone other than himself (the growing fetus) has an impact on her.

Statement 32: Children need their father even if he is violent.

This statement is FALSE. The statement is a myth that keeps many women in a dangerous relationship "for the sake of the children." Studies show that most children suffer permanent damage from viewing violence (J.S. Cummings et al., 1981). They may themselves become victimizers of others or may allow themselves to be victimized.

CULTURAL ISSUES

Statement 5: Unlike poorer women, middle-class women are not likely to get battered.

Statement 7: Minority women are battered more frequently than Anglo women.

Statement 11: Battered women are uneducated and have few job skills.

These statements are all FALSE. Most studies indicate that battering occurs across socioeconomic, racial, ethnic, and educational levels. A battered woman is everywoman. She may come from any walk of life and is as likely to be a successful professional woman as a ghetto dweller (Gelles & Straus, 1989). It is certainly the case, however, that poorer women who are battered are more likely to come to the attention of the authorities than are wealthier women. For one thing, a battering incident happening to a woman who lives in a poorly built apartment with thin walls is more likely to be heard by neighbors than is the beating received by a woman whose closest neighbor lives in the mansion a mile down the road.

Statement 9:   *Religious beliefs strongly decrease the probability of becoming a batterer.*

This statement is also FALSE. As indicated previously, battering does not discriminate; it can happen to any woman. Belonging to a certain religious group does not protect a woman from being battered or prevent a man from battering her (Gelles & Straus, 1989). Battering is just as likely to occur in Christian homes as in Jewish ones; in homes where religiosity is a big focus of the family as well as in homes where religiosity is nonexistent.

DYNAMICS OF BATTERING

Statement 12:   *Alcohol causes battering when the man drinks.*

Although many batterers are also alcoholics or problem drinkers, research indicates that men who abuse alcohol tend to do most of their battering when sober (Browne, 1987; Gelles & Straus, 1989). Even when battering under the influence of alcohol, the alcohol cannot be blamed for the battering, even though alcoholic batterers will often blame the violence on the drinking. In fact, when these men are treated for alcoholism and cease drinking, they continue to abuse their partners, unless the battering too is treated. Thus the preceding statement is FALSE.

---

*Statement 6:   Twenty percent of all Americans approve of
                 hitting a spouse on appropriate occasions.*

Study results indicate that the statement above is TRUE
(Straus et al., 1980). An impressive segment of the American
population does think that under certain circumstances it is
appropriate to hit a spouse. Of course, this finding is not
surprising when you consider that until late in the last cen-
tury it was considered the responsibility of the husband to
use corporal punishment since "It is better to punish the body
and correct the soul than to damage the soul and spare the
body . . . readily beat her, not in rage but out of charity and
concern for her soul" (quoted in Davidson, 1978, p. 99). In
fact, a commonly used colloquial expression "the rule of
thumb" comes from English case law that gave a husband
permission to hit his wife with a rod no wider than the width
of a thumb (Hart, 1993).

Statement 13:   Batterers are violent in all their relationships.

Statement 22:   A wife batterer also beats his children.

These statements are TRUE and also FALSE. Batterers
are usually not violent in relationships at work or with others outside the home. However, a batterer is likely to be abusive in relationships with others. Also, although many
batterers are not violent with their children, in 30% to 70% of
cases in which there is spouse abuse there is also child physical or sexual abuse (Hughes, 1982; Pagelow, 1989; Straus et
al., 1980).

---

*Statement 14:   Batterers are unsuccessful and lack resources
                 to cope with the world.*

Statement 17:   Batterers have psychopathic personalities.

These statements are FALSE. Just as researchers have
been unsuccessful in developing a profile of the typical bat-

tered woman, developing a profile of the typical batterer has been difficult. All kinds of men batter, successful as well as unsuccessful men (Edleson, Eisikovits, & Guttman, 1985; Hotaling & Sugarman, 1986). Although most batterers do not demonstrate any differences from other men on personality tests, researchers have found that a subset of batterers can indeed be classified as psychopathic; however, these men are also those who have been in trouble with the law in a variety of venues.

Statement 21: *The batterer is not a loving partner.*

Statement 40: *Battering usually occurs when the husband's feelings of love for his partner are replaced by anger and hate.*

These statements are both FALSE. Although it may be difficult to think of someone who can beat his wife senseless as a loving partner, the reality of living with a batterer is that he can often be an extremely loving and charming partner. Some researchers have described the Dr. Jekyll and Mr. Hyde nature of the batterer (Walker, 1979). Indeed, Lenore Walker explains the changes by describing the three phases of the violence cycle. The first phase includes the build-up of tension. This is inevitably followed by the explosion of violence (Phase 2 or battering phase). The third phase has been described as the honeymoon phase when the batterer once again becomes the charming, loving man the woman fell in love with. During this phase, the batterer expresses contriteness for his outburst and often courts his partner with flowers and other romantic gestures. During this phase, the batterer appears to be a very loving partner. Throughout the cycle of violence, most batterers maintain that they continue to love their partners.

Statement 30:   Batterers will cease their violence once the couple gets married.

Statement 31:   In a battering relationship, often the batterer spontaneously stops being violent permanently, if he is happier.

Both of these statements are FALSE. If a man is violent prior to marriage, it is likely that the violence will increase once the couple gets married. Battering escalates and needs to be treated. It is a common misconception of women who are battered that if they could only figure out how to make their mates happier (or if only his job situation got better, or if he could better control his drinking) then the violence would cease. The battering must be acknowledged as a characteristic of the batterer and not as something the woman has much control over, and it must be treated for it to cease (Hansen & Harway, 1993).

Statement 37:   Signs that a partner will become a batterer are usually present in the first few weeks of the relationship.

FALSE. There are no consistent patterns regarding when abuse first appears or how it manifests. Violence may occur early in the relationship or take some time to develop. Usually, there has been a progression of abuse from verbal to increasingly violent physical abuse over some extended period of time.

ASSESSMENT AND TREATMENT ISSUES

Statement 15:   The most important goal in working with a battered woman is to help her leave the abusive partner.

This statement is FALSE. After making sure that a battered woman is safe, empowerment is the primary goal of psychotherapy (Brown, 1991). The therapist must be willing to let her make her own decision about whether to leave or stay with the batterer. If she decides to leave, therapist and client must be apprised of the fact that this period is probably the most dangerous for the battered woman. Indeed, many batterers become desperate when they are threatened with abandonment and are at their most dangerous then.

Statement 34: *When a woman leaves an abusive relationship, the likelihood of serious injury increases.*

This is TRUE. Studies show an increase in violence when the woman attempts to leave her husband (Giles-Sims, 1983). Both threats and actual attacks increase in number and the danger of a lethal outcome is highest when the woman tries to leave (Browne, 1987).

Statement 24: *Once a battered woman, always a battered woman.*

Statement 25: *Once a batterer, always a batterer.*

The first statement is FALSE, the second TRUE under most circumstances. Most battered women who leave a battering relationship go on to establish good relationships. Thus, battered women will not necessarily repeatedly pick men who batter. At the same time, men who batter, unless they are treated for partner abuse, are likely to go on to additional battering relationships (U.S. Commission on Civil Rights, 1982). Batterers who are not treated are likely to simply cycle women: As one refuses to put up with the abuse, he simply finds another whom he can control, at least for some time. This is because battering is not the result of a dysfunctional relationship, but rather the result of an individual man's dysfunctional relational style (Hansen & Harway, 1993).

Statement 28: The diagnostic clue "accident prone" may appear in the history of some women.

This statement is TRUE. Battered women are reluctant to reveal their abuse, because they have been made to feel responsible for it by society and persons from whom they might have previously sought help. However, women who have been battered repeatedly over time may have a history of many "accidents" in which they broke bones, sprained backs, tore ligaments, or had extensive contusions (Warshaw, 1989). This type of history should always be investigated for evidence of battering.

Statement 35: The majority of battered women have been hit 1 to 3 times by their partner before being successfully helped.

This statement is FALSE. The majority of battered women secretly endure abuse for years and may never receive help (Okun, 1986).

Statement 38: Upon hearing that a woman is in an abusive relationship, the majority of mental health professionals are most concerned about the woman's safety.

Unfortunately this statement is FALSE. Mental health professionals should be most concerned about the woman's safety upon assessing that she is being battered. However, two recent studies (Hansen et al., 1991; Harway & Hansen, 1990) suggest otherwise. Most mental health professionals do not focus first on the woman's safety but rather are more concerned with issues such as the couple's interpersonal dynamics. Clearly more training is needed to insure that battered women are adequately treated. As Goodstein and Page's research (1991) indicates, if the battering is not identified and dealt with immediately, it is unlikely that the woman will return for a second session.

LEGAL AND ETHICAL ISSUES

Statement 10: *If spouse abuse is suspected, mental health professionals are required by law to report it to the authorities.*

This statement is FALSE. There are no domestic violence mandated reporting laws for mental health practitioners in the United States, unless the abused individual is a minor, an elder (over 65), or a dependent adult, or if the clinician is working in a medical setting in California. However, when the battered woman is underage or elderly or physically or emotionally dependent on a caretaker, then mental health professionals are mandated to report the violence (to the Department of Children's Services or the Department of Social Services in California; to other departments in other jurisdictions; Cervantes, 1993).

Statement 18: *In most parts of the country, police have been unsuccessful in protecting a battered woman.*

This statement is TRUE. A woman who has been battered may go to court to obtain a restraining order against her abuser. In some jurisdictions, this makes it easier for the police to arrest a batterer who is in violation of the order (Hart, 1993). However, the restraining order is only a piece of paper, and a batterer who is determined to harm his partner can do so. The police can only help when they are on the premises. In fact, police indicate that domestic violence calls are dangerous to them as well as to the woman.

Statement 39: The majority of abused senior citizens are beaten by their partners.

TRUE. A number of recent articles suggest that many elder abuse victims are abused by their spouses and some have suffered from years of chronic abuse (Ramsey-Klawsnik, 1993; Pillemer & Suitor, 1991). Although spouse abuse is not reportable in most jurisdictions, spouse abuse when the spouse is over 65 is reportable under elder abuse reporting statutes.

3

Assessment of
Spouse Abuse

How does a clinician know that the individual or couple presenting for therapy with a variety of presenting problems actually is experiencing spouse abuse? Spouse abuse is both difficult and very easy to assess. It can be relatively easy to assess for spouse abuse if you know the psychological characteristics that abused women present (men are sometimes the abused one, but quite rarely). Likewise, violent couples also come to therapy with telltale signs that an abuse-sensitized therapist can easily identify. Identifying abuse may be difficult for other therapists for other reasons. First, the client is unlikely to specifically address the violence as a presenting issue. Most abused women may be experiencing substantial denial. These women will resist the abuse label even after you have applied it to her circumstances. It is rare that the woman will present information about violence to you at intake, even if you ask her directly. However, if violence is not addressed, many clients will not return for a second visit (Goodstein & Page, 1981)

Second, the abused woman may initially be afraid to describe what she recognizes as violence, particularly in the presence of her husband. Third, abused women may be embarrassed and believe that you will think less of them for staying in the abusive relationship.

In this section, we will discuss how to assess for the existence of spouse abuse. We will separately discuss how to make this assessment when the woman presents as the client, when the man presents separately, when the couple or family come in for treatment, and when the children are brought in.

ASSESSING THE
WOMAN FOR SPOUSE ABUSE

DOES VIOLENCE EXIST?

> Mary Ann, a 38-year-old accountant, has sought therapy for depression. She describes her behavior as lethargic and unmotivated, having some difficulty sleeping at night and easily teary. Mary Ann is married with three children, stably employed for the last 10 years. Her husband, Jim, 42, an engineer, is said to be a good provider, a good father, and a loyal mate.

Even though you are not aware of it at the time, Mary Ann is a typical battered woman. A battered woman is likely to present for therapy complaining about everything else, but never mentioning that she is in a violent relationship. How then does the therapist know to assess for violence and evaluate the specific needs of the client? Some excerpts from Mary Ann's intake interview demonstrate a possible approach.

Therapist: Tell me some more about your tiredness and trouble sleeping. How long have these problems been going on?

Mary Ann: For some time now. But recently they have gotten worse. And it's starting to affect my ability to do my job.

Therapist: Why now? Has something happened recently that has been bothering you?

Mary Ann: Nothing really new. I do worry about my children.

Therapist: Oh? Why is that?

Mary Ann: (whispers) I'm afraid about what they see or hear.

Therapist: Is there something specific?

Mary Ann: (quietly) Not really.

Therapist: Tell me about your relationship with Jim.

Mary Ann: Jim is a good father and a good provider. He doesn't drink or smoke. He's in good physical shape. As far as I know he's always been faithful to me.

Therapist: How would you describe your marriage?

Mary Ann: Okay. No different from others, I guess.

Therapist: All relationships are special. What's special about yours?

Mary Ann: It's really pretty average. But I guess others seem to have more fun. We're always arguing.

Therapist: Is that why you're not sleeping?

Mary Ann: Well, I keep thinking about it. . . .

Therapist: Tell me about your most recent argument.

Mary Ann: I wanted to buy a new couch for the family room and Jim told me that we couldn't afford it. Now we both bring in pretty good salaries and I know we have $8,000 in a savings account. So, I couldn't understand why Jim would say we can't afford it. We have had the same couch now for 12 years and the entire right side is ripped. It's embarrassing.

Therapist: So, what happened?

Mary Ann: We kept arguing and (she begins to cry). . . .

Therapist: (hands tissue) and then. . . .

Mary Ann: I'm so tired of struggling, for everything. Even a measly couch!

Therapist: And. . . .

Mary Ann: (barely audibly) He called me a bitch and told me that no wonder I have no friends. That nobody could ever stand me. Then he pushed the coffee table over and he broke my best Wedgewood candy holder. Then he slapped me.

Therapist: That seems like quite a strong reaction! He struck you. . . .

Mary Ann: Yes . . . but not too hard.

Therapist: He struck you harder before?

Mary Ann: Well, yes. . . .

The intake interview may not always provide evidence that violence is present in the client's relationship, as readily as presented here. All intake interviews should include questions about conflict and violence in the relationship, even where there is otherwise no evidence of violence (just as more therapists routinely ask about alcohol and drug abuse). A direct question such as "Has your husband (partner) ever hit you?" may not yield relevant information. She may answer "No," partly because of her shame in being the recipient of physical abuse, but also because she may have been pushed, had objects thrown at her, or had weapons pointed at her and thus technically may not have been "hit" by her husband. Instead, a series of questions directed at the couple's style of conflict resolution may be more effective. That is why our therapist asked about the couple's most recent disagreement. The therapist might also have asked: "How do you and your husband deal with disagreements?" Alternately she might have asked: "When your husband is extremely upset with you, what does he say and do?" or "In any of these disagreements, has your husband ever touched you physically?" (to be followed by inquiries about pushing, physically holding her down, or whether he has used his body or any type of instrument to strike or physically hurt her). The therapist might instead have asked: "Has your husband ever been abusive with you, either verbally or physically?"

There are a number of different ways of putting forth these or similar questions. First, it is important to be sensitive to the characteristics of shame, guilt, embarrassment, and fear that may prevent the woman from responding to direct questioning. Sensitivity and persistence are essential. Second, it is important to recognize that a single question may not yield very reliable information about the presence or absence of violence and of the possible danger to the woman. Third, it is important to persevere and ask follow-up questions even though the woman denies any violence in her relationship. As the self-quiz earlier pointed out (see Chapter 2), women who ended up in hospital emergency rooms after being battered had previously seen a therapist, but only for one session and the therapist *never asked about the violence*. An alert therapist will err on the side of thoroughness when inquiring about spousal abuse.

Many abused women may complete the intake interview convincing you that they have not experienced violence. These women have acquired characteristics that serve both to protect them and keep them in their abusive relationships. Follingstad et al. (1988) describe the variety of coping styles that battered women might adopt in coming to terms with the abuse. These coping styles allow the woman to survive the battering, but serve to insure that she remains in the abusive relationship. One style of coping involves the woman's own conceptualization of why the abuse has occurred. Among the conceptualizations acquired by battered women to understand the battering are (a) denial of the seriousness of the injury she has experienced, (b) attribution of the blame for the violence to forces outside the control of both partners,

(c) blaming herself for the violence, (d) denial of her emotional or practical options, (e) wanting to save her partner by
helping him overcome his problem while continuing to toler-
ate the abuse, and (f) her commitment to enduring the violence for the sake of some higher commitment such as religion or tradition (Ferraro & Johnson, 1983). The battered
woman's denial in the face of your persistent inquiry may be
a clear signal that she is not yet ready to address the characteristics of the abusive relationship. However, you are ethi-
cally bound to provide appropriate treatment, because your
client may also be in physical danger. Therefore, it is important for you to know that your client is being abused.

When persistent inquiry fails to inform you of violence
in a relationship, alternative approaches are available. Battered women often share a number of presenting characteristics with other survivors of trauma. Globally, these characteristics have been described as those of Post-Traumatic Stress
Disorder (PTSD). These symptoms may include depression
(which might be the result of a common coping mechanism
of battered women: Expressing anger toward the batterer
could well have the effect of increasing the violence. In con-
trast, repressing the intense anger experienced in response to
a beating may instead have greater survival value); reexperi-
encing the trauma through nightmares, flashbacks, and/or
intrusive thoughts of the trauma; numbing to the external
world and a variety of anxiety-related symptoms such as sleep
disturbance, eating disorders, or substance abuse; and avoidance of stimuli associated with the trauma and an intensifica-
tion of anxiety when confronted with reminders of the trauma.
Other presenting characteristics may be a diminished
decision-making and problem-solving style (attributed by researchers to repeated exposure to the trauma), suicidality,
somatization, hypervigilance, emotional lability, and victimization of others. (See Table 1, p. 41.)

Psychotherapists working with battered women may be
surprised to see the woman blaming herself for causing the

TABLE 1:

Common PTSD Symptoms Found Among Battered Women

Depression	Suicidality
Anxiety	Intrusive Thoughts
Sleep Disorders	Somatization
Eating Disorders	Victimization of Others
Substance Abuse	Hypervigilance

abuse. They may also notice that she blames herself for not being able to modify the occurrence of the abuse or for tolerating the abuse. However, this coping style is described by Miller and Porter (1983) as allowing the woman to maintain the illusion that she is still in control of her life. She is therefore allowed to believe that a "just world" exists where people get what they deserve and bad things do not happen to good people. Unfortunately her perception of control and a just world often serve to keep her in the abusive situation and frustrates the efforts of those who would encourage her to leave. In support of this position, Hendricks-Matthews (1982) reports that therapy is less successful for women who self-blame than for those who blame their batterers.

After the initial battering incident, the woman often sees the violence as an aberration and as something that she may be able to control. She then focuses on identifying ways of preventing the abuse from recurring. Eventually, she may become discouraged. Some research suggests that battered women have a significantly higher external locus of control than a normative sample, or a belief that she has little impact on her fate. Battered women who are in longer relationships appear to have a higher external locus of control than battered women in shorter relationships (Cheney & Bleker, 1982). Similarly, Feldman (1983) found that battered women who continued in their relationships had a more external locus of control than did either battered women who left the relationship or women not in battering relationships. This research suggests that there may be characteristics about being in or continuing in abusive relationships that erode a woman's sense of control over her own destiny and ultimately result in the passivity or numbness that some have reported in battered women (see Hanks & Rosenbaum, 1977, or Walker's, 1984 explanations of the battered woman syndrome and learned helplessness).

You may choose to use an abuse inventory (e.g., the Abuse Risk Inventory published by Consulting Psychologist Press; Hudson & McIntosh's [1981] Index of Spouse Abuse; Bodin's [1992] Relationship Conflict Inventory) or some other screening test to insure that all presenting symptoms of spouse abuse are recognized.

Your first task as a clinician, then, is to identify the violence experienced by a client who may not be forthcoming with the information about her abuse. You would be wise to keep in mind the possibility of domestic violence with all clients who present with some or all of the constellation of presenting characteristics listed previously.

HOW DANGEROUS IS THE VIOLENCE?

As discussed before, the therapist's first task is to identify whether violence is a factor for the client. The therapist's next task is to ascertain the level of danger that the client faces. Epidemiological research of domestic violence clearly indicates that conjugal assaults tend to have more serious consequences than other types of assault (see Harway & Hansen, 1993a, for more detailed statistics). Many women endure repeated batterings, often of increasing severity, within a relatively short time frame (e.g., in one study [Okun, 1986], women experienced more than five assaults every 4 weeks, with 20% being battered twice or more per week). The injuries that battered women report range from lacerations and fractures to bullet and stab wounds. In many cases, domestic violence is extreme enough to result in murder; lethality in cases of wife battering is most likely to occur when the woman tries to leave (Browne, 1987).

These statistics make it imperative for you to assess the danger to the client early in treatment. Questions about the existence of weapons within the home must be asked. Likewise, you should obtain a detailed battering history about the use or threat of use of weapons, including common household weapons such as carving knives and the like. The progression of the abuse should also be documented. Seldom does domestic violence begin in the most severe form. Usually there is a pattern of increasingly severe emotional abuse which may include insults, name-calling, demeaning comments, threats, and accusations, or intense questioning about normal daily activities. Isolation and intimidation may be used. The man may have used his physical presence or size or threatened her with violence (e.g., standing in the doorway so that she is unable to leave; taking her car keys, money, checkbook, or credit cards so that she cannot leave; unplugging the phone so she cannot call police, friends, or family). At some point, the emotional and verbal abuse may have graduated to the use of physical objects as threats (e.g., throwing objects, breaking personal items, tearing clothes, or driving recklessly to scare her). The physical violence may begin with pushing and shoving which then can lead to slapping, biting, choking, hair pulling, kicking, backhanding, punching, and eventually to the use of weapons. Not every batterer will necessarily follow the same pattern, nor will each situation of abuse graduate to the same behaviors. However, you need to be aware of the possibilities of such incremental changes in the violence.

Assessing the extent of danger the client is in must be ongoing. You have a responsibility to be aware of the potential danger to the client at each step in the therapy.

HOW SEVERELY AFFECTED IS THE CLIENT?

The third and final level of assessment that must be considered in the treatment of the battered woman concerns the impact of the abuse on the client. The TRIADS model developed by Burgess, Hartman, and Kelly (1990) may be useful to consider. TRIADS is a trauma assessment tool of more general utility than assessing for battering. Useful for all types of trauma, it gives clinicians a quick sense of the extent of emotional injury experienced by the battered woman.

TRIADS is an acronym for *T*ypes of abuse (physical, sexual, psychological), *R*ole relationships between victim and offender (intrafamilial vs. extrafamilial), *I*ntensity (number of acts and offenders), *A*ffective state (expressed vs. controlled demeanor), *D*uration (length of time), and *S*tyle of abuse (single, patterned, or ritualistic). To the extent that a woman has been abused both physically and psychologically as well as forced to engage in sex acts against her will by a spouse or life partner repeatedly (especially after a prior history of abuse) and over a long period of time, she is likely to be most damaged. Her affective state will also indicate the extent of damage, in that a client who is overly controlled is likely to be more affected than a client who is emotionally labile. Not every woman will experience Post-Traumatic Stress Disorder, but it is important to assess this early so that proper treatment can be implemented.

The assessment of impact of abuse on a woman's functioning should be made whether she is currently in the abusive relationship or recently removed from it, as she is likely to have symptoms for some time after leaving the abusive relationship.

ASSESSING THE
MAN FOR SPOUSE ABUSE

The batterer rarely presents in therapy of his own volition. He is much more likely to seek therapy only when court referred subsequent to a violent episode or when referred by his wife as the result of an ultimatum prior to divorce. Because of the referral modality, it will be clear when a batterer presents for therapy.

How then should you identify a male client who enters therapy for some reason other than battering? The research on batterer characteristics and typologies concludes that for the most part there is no clear batterer profile (Gondolf, 1993). Identifying batterers based on symptomatology or characteristics may be difficult. Gondolf recommends assessing how the client reacts to control and anger cues. (O'Neil & Egan [1993] suggest that the clinician assess whether the male client is in gender-role conflict. This manifests as rigid, sexist, or restrictive gender-role socialization which may present as restrictive emotionality and with a focus on power and competition issues. In particular, key is the assessment of the man's perception of power conflicts as internal, caused by others, or expressed by others.)

> Tom, 48, is a successful physician. He has been married for 10 years to Ellen, 39, who prior to their marriage was employed as an operating room nurse. This is Tom's second marriage, Ellen's first. They have no children of their own, although Tom has grown twin boys from a prior marriage. Tom has entered therapy because he is worried that Ellen may

be having an affair and his best friend has recommended therapy as the way to get some ideas about
how to handle the situation. A first interview with
Tom indicates that Tom is convinced that he has been
an excellent husband and that Ellen's lack of responsiveness to his sexual advances is because she is involved with someone else. He describes her as having become increasingly distant to him and can identify nothing in his own behavior or their relationship which can account for the changes. He also
indicates that Ellen has been more reluctant of late
to keep up with her household responsibilities and
with the help she has always provided to him in his
medical office. During the intake interview, Tom
repeatedly blames her for the changes which have
taken place and states "If she would only have lis-
tened to me and not taken the course at the University, none of this would have happened. She has
responsibilities and she is not living up to these as
we had agreed."

Spousal abuse may have roots in gender-roles, because
men's gender-role socialization teaches them that being masculine means maintaining power over women. They may use
power over their life partners in destructive and often violent
ways, to the extent that their masculine identity is dependent
on this belief system. Thus, identifying a man's belief about
gender-roles is likely to provide important clues as to his likelihood to embark on psychologically or physically abusive
paths.

Segel-Evans (1994) provides other important clues to a
man's potential for violence. In describing the cycle of violence first popularized by Lenore Walker (1979), Segel-Evans
explains the dynamics of the tension build-up phase. He indicates that this phase is the result of feelings defended against;
for example, the man may experience guilt or shame about

something either in the present or the past, fear abandonment, or simply feel hurt. His inability to experience his feelings leads in turn to one or more defenses against those feelings, for example, abuse of alcohol or drugs, the search for negative excitement, *or* blaming his spouse. The use of alcohol or drugs may defuse the underlying unrecognized feelings. Similarly, blaming the spouse—who is quickly seen as the enemy— leads to attacking that enemy (Walker's explosion phase) which in turn releases the built-up tension. This explosion is then followed by what Walker describes as the honeymoon period. Inevitably, since life brings with it many problems, tension will build up again and the cycle will continue to repeat itself because of the batterer's inability to take responsibility for his own feelings (or even to recognize them). Thus, another diagnostic sign that you may look for is a man's inability to recognize his feelings and his externalization of the blame for the things that happen to him. These characteristics will not in all cases signify a violent man. However, they are important styles to attend to. Segel-Evans describes the cycle as one where the man attempts to control and where, regardless of what the other party does, the cycle continues. He also indicates that an abuser may be violent only in his intimate relationships, but he will also be controlling and abusive in most of his relationships. Thus, you may well find it useful to identify how a man who is suspected of being violent behaves in other more distant relationships, including how the abuser responds to the therapist.

ASSESSING A COUPLE FOR VIOLENCE

When a couple presents for marital counseling, the clinician is faced with the most difficult task of all in terms of assessing for the presence and severity of violence. A recent study by Holtzworth-Munroe et al. (1992) indicates that a his-

tory of marital violence is present in far more maritally distressed couples than are otherwise identified. Thus, the therapist who sees a couple for otherwise run-of-the-mill marital
problems must always assess for spousal abuse. This assessment is complicated by the fact that a battered woman, even
one not in denial, would be unlikely (even unwise) to reveal
the violence in the presence of her batterer. She may fear (often legitimately) that she would suffer the consequences after the session. For this reason, you should always conduct
intake interviews with couples in such a way that at least some
portion of the intake is spent alone with each partner. The
battered woman is more likely to provide an accurate account
of the conflict, including revealing her abuse (or to specify
the severity of abuse if the couple presents because of the violence), if she is alone in the room with you. The information
is elicited from her using the same types of questions described
in the section relating to assessment of the single woman client. If battering is reported in this individual interview by
the woman, the dilemma of the therapist becomes what to do
with the information. In order to insure the continued well-
being of the woman, you cannot overtly implement a treatment plan that focuses on the violence or refers to the violence when the couple is reunited in session (to do so would
endanger the woman and make her vulnerable to a battering
after the session). As we will describe later, the initial treatment of choice with a violent couple is not to work in a couples
modality. Thus, at the end of this intake session, some ration-
ale, other than the violence, must be given for your decision
to treat the couple in individual therapy. One of the dilem-
mas of working in this modality with a violent couple is that
the battered woman, with treatment, will inevitably become
stronger. As she becomes empowered she is likely to face
greater physical danger. (This point will be discussed in
greater detail under the treatment section.) Initial goals of
the batterer's treatment will be to help him recognize and

openly acknowledge his violence. Until he does so, the information gained from the woman (individually at intake) must continue to be protected. Of course, only then can the real treatment of the battering behavior begin.

ASSESSING CHILDREN FOR THE EFFECTS OF SPOUSAL ABUSE

Battered women often state that they are staying married to their abuser "because of the children." These women believe that the effects of a divorce would be worse on the children than those of watching or hearing the battering their mother undergoes. There is a great deal of evidence that being exposed to spousal violence has profound effects on children, both in the short term and over the longer term.

Children suffering from the effects of exposure to spousal abuse may come into therapy as part of a family seeking family therapy or may be brought in by parents alarmed by the symptoms the children evidence. In either case, the parents are unlikely to specify that there is violence in the family at the time of the initial contact with the therapist.

You, therefore, will have to rely on your diagnostic powers in making an assessment about violence in the family as a precipitator for the children's behavior. It will be particularly important for you to be aware of the types of presentation which may suggest battering (unfortunately, these types of presentations are also common to many other familial or individual dysfunctions). Children who are exposed to background violence may present with increased emotional arousal, distress, and increased aggressiveness. With repeated exposure, the child may develop acute sensitivity to all expressions of anger and may misinterpret many cues as aggressive when they are not. School performance may suffer with increased distractibility and inattentiveness (Jaffe, Wolfe, & Wilson, 1990).

Children are most often brought in for therapy by their parents and most often by their mother. Parents who are experiencing abuse may be more comfortable obtaining help for their child than for themselves. Women who state that they are staying with their husband for the sake of the children may become concerned when their children begin to exhibit disruptive behaviors or symptoms of anxiety and depression. Research on children who have witnessed spouse abuse indicates that the immediate impact is more likely to be seen in the sons of the abuser than in the daughters. These sons have been noted to exhibit symptoms of aggression toward peers, siblings, and their mothers (Berman, 1993). They may also exhibit signs of depression and anxiety. Daughters who witness abuse are more likely to demonstrate increased problems with depression and anxiety, though they, too, may appear more aggressive than girls who have not been exposed to battering. Eventually, children exposed to violence are likely to adopt one of three patterns of functioning (Berman, 1993): (a) responding with anger and aggression toward others—dubbed the victimizer, (b) responding with passivity and powerlessness—assuming the victim role, or (c) responding with resilience.

Current approaches to therapy with children often include an initial interview with the parent and the child and a subsequent interview with the child alone. An initial interview with the child is appropriate even if you intend to work collaterally with the parent and the child. Spouse abuse is often a covert family secret, and the child may feel disloyal to the family if encouraged to share this secret with the therapist. The therapist, therefore, must invest in establishing a trusting relationship with the child and approach the subject of spousal violence from the perspective of the child "helping the family."

The following is a sample from an initial interview: Charley in this case is 7 years old.

Therapist: I wanted to spend a few minutes getting to know you better. What do you like to do when you're not in school? What kind of (music, movies, TV, etc.) do you like? . . . What's your favorite program?

Charley: (responds)

Therapist: Mine too, did you see the one when . . . (spends time connecting and provides child an opportunity to connect).

Therapist: Your Mom seems pretty concerned about you. She says the teacher said you're not paying attention in school, kind of daydreaming. Do you like school? . . . When your mind wanders, and you don't pay attention, what are you thinking about?

Charley: I don't know . . . nothin'. . . .

Therapist: Everybody's thinking about something, are you thinking about not being in school . . . being home . . . about your parents?

Charley: Sometimes. . . .

Therapist: Lots of kids think about their parents, which one do you worry about the most?

Charley: My Mom. . . .

Therapist: Why's that? Why do you worry more about your Mom than your Dad?

Charley: I worry about my Dad too but my Dad's strong . . . I don't know. . . .

Therapist: Yeah he is big and strong . . . does he scare you?

Charley: Sometimes. . . .

Therapist: When does he scare you?

Charley: When he yells. . . .

Therapist: Does he yell a lot?

Charley: Yeah, but more at my Mom than me and my little brother. . . .

Therapist: Your Dad yells at your Mom a lot . . . What do you do?

Charley: I take my little brother and we hide in the room. I don't want to hear it.

Therapist   It sounds pretty scary!

Charley: Yeah.

Therapist: What else are you afraid of? Do you ever get afraid your parents might get a divorce?

Charley: Well, yeah, kinda. . . .

Therapist: Why are you afraid your parents might get a divorce? Is that what you worry about in school?

Charley: Yeah, they've been fighting a lot lately. . . .

Therapist: Yelling and stuff?

Charley: Yeah. . . .

Therapist: Are you in the room?

Charley: Sometimes . . . I can always hear them through the wall. . . .

Therapist: What do you hear?

Charley: She tells him she's going to leave and . . . (stops, becomes quiet).

Therapist: What is it?

Charley: Nothin'. . . .

Therapist: I bet you're afraid of telling on Dad. . . .

Charley: Sorta. . . .

Therapist: Charley, you can really help your family by telling what goes on. What happens when your Dad gets really angry? Does your Dad ever get so mad, he gets violent?

Charley: (hesitating) Sometimes. . . .

Therapist: What happens?

Charley: (hesitating) One time. . . .

Therapist: Yes?

Charley: . . . he pushed my Mom down and I ran out of the house to get the neighbors.

At this point you can explore the violence in greater detail. Specifics are important, particularly concerning the frequency and severity of the abuse. Is the violence daily; were weapons used; did the child observe marks on the mother the day after the violence occurred? Also, what did the mother do to resolve the violence? Did she ever go to the hospital? Did she go to a shelter? Did she contact relatives or friends? You need to reassure the child that you will attempt to help the family. Often children perceive themselves as somehow responsible for the father's anger, or responsible for protecting the mother. If divorce or separation is imminent, the child may take on the responsibility for the ultimate breakup of the family.

In a home where spousal abuse is chronic, you must also carefully assess whether concurrent child abuse might also be happening. Research suggests that this is likely in as many as 30% to 70% of cases (Hughes, 1982; Pagelow, 1989; Straus et al., 1980). In such a situation, of course, the mandated reporting requirements surrounding child abuse are brought into play.

Early intervention is critical. Assessing a child who is brought in for therapy when spousal violence is suspected should always include direct questioning of the parents about the occurrence of violence in the home. Working with the mother to help educate her to the negative effects on the child of viewing spousal violence will not only serve to empower the woman, but may also give her the additional motivation she needs to remove herself and her children from an abusive situation.

A LAST WORD ON ASSESSMENT

In this chapter, we have been discussing how the clinician might assess for the existence of violence in intact families. Part of the task of the therapist, however, is to assess for the long-term impact of domestic violence even where an intact family does not present for treatment. Consequently, part of any good assessment should be the evaluation of the context: Which members of the family present for therapy, who is being treated, and what constitutes the family. Although a couple may be divorced, if the father still has ongoing contact with his children during visitation, treatment should consider whether he remains a danger to the family and what impact he continues to have on individual and family functioning. As a result, treatment of family members must consider father's role even if he is not physically present in the therapy room. Moreover, in many cases, the husband's disappearance from the scene may not by itself signal the end of symptoms caused by his abuse. Family members should be assessed for Post-Traumatic Stress Disorder or other long-term consequences of abuse.

4

Treatment of Spouse Abuse

THE INDIVIDUAL WOMAN

As noted in Chapter 3, the battered woman rarely comes into treatment presenting with battering as her primary concern. Helping the client identify the parameters of the violence she is experiencing can be a useful introductory phase of therapy. Therapy with the individual woman may continue with crisis intervention, short-term therapy, and long-term therapy (see Table 2, "Overview of a Treatment Model for Working With Battered Women," p. 58).

CRISIS INTERVENTION

The first major goal of treatment with battered women is always to address issues of safety. The safety of the woman and her children must be insured before any additional interventions can occur. Crisis intervention may also include addressing practical issues such as finances, housing, and legal assistance.

Crisis intervention and the development of a safety plan must begin with the first session, as often battered women do not return for additional treatment (Goodstein & Page, 1981). Therefore, you must address safety within this first session as if circumstances will prevent the client from returning for

TABLE 2:

Overview of a Treatment Model for Working With Battered Women

Phase I—Crisis Intervention

A. Assess for the existence of violence

B. Assess the danger the woman is in

C. Educate the woman about battering and domestic violence and validate her experience

D. Develop and practice a safety or danger-management plan

Phase II—Short-term counseling

A. Work on empowerment issues

B. Develop independent living skills and attitudes

C. Help client grieve the loss of the idealized relationship

Phase III—Long-term counseling

A. Heal the past

B. Develop trust

C. Work from a trauma recovery model to heal resulting psychological problems

additional treatment. Some clients are at particular risk for battering which may attain lethal proportions (see Table 3, "Assessing for Lethality," p. 59).

TABLE 3:

Assessing for Lethality

Key factors to assess in determining whether the batterer has the potential to kill:

- Threats of homicide or suicide

- Acute depression and hopelessness

- Possession of weapons

- Obsessiveness about partner or family, beliefs that he cannot live without them or that they are the center of his universe

- Rage

- Drug or alcohol consumption combined with despair

- History of pet abuse

- Easy access to the battered woman and/or family members

The presence of the preceding indicators increases the likelihood that the batterer is contemplating killing or committing life-endangering violence.

Many therapists working with battered women tell of the creative safety plans of their clients: A battered woman might slowly and gradually remove vital items from the home over a period of weeks or months. Then, the day she finally leaves, she is completely prepared to begin a new life with all the necessary economic and physical resources. She may also choose to leave a note or a message on the answering machine rather than speak to her partner directly.

You should help the client develop a safety plan if she has not developed one of her own. The major goal of a safety plan is to decrease the likelihood that the woman will be physically harmed during the next violent episode. Providing safety may include teaching her techniques to deescalate her partner's violence while insuring that she does not feel responsible for his violence. In addition, a safety plan may include establishing recognizable criteria for physically leaving the batterer's presence when he is violent. Some of the elements of the safety plan (Register, 1993) may include discussion of the following:

1. how to predict that violence is imminent

2. how to physically leave the situation (i.e., identification and rehearsal of an exit route)

3. exploration of whether safety is best provided by a brief or more lengthy departure

4. preparation of a safety kit that includes items necessary for survival upon departure (e.g., clothing, medication, money, car keys) to be kept near the exit route

5. arrangements for shelter, lodging, or friends who will provide a safe haven (in all instances, the shelter arrangements should be made so that the batterer will not know of the woman's whereabouts)

You should proceed with caution if your recommendation is that the client leave the batterer. Many batterers threaten to kill their wife if she leaves and this threat needs to be taken seriously because the risk of death increases when the battered woman leaves her abuser (Browne, 1987). In addition, men who kill their wives and then themselves are more likely to do so during the period of separation or divorce (Price & Hansen, 1991). Therefore, if the client's partner threatens that he will kill himself if she were to leave, she must be concerned for her own safety and the safety of her children as well. Although you may personally believe that *all* women should leave *all* men who batter, keeping a woman safe when she leaves a batterer is a difficult task.

Most battered women who leave the batterer return to him and are then at greater risk of injury. The battered woman who eventually leaves returns six to seven times on average before she makes her final move (Browne, 1987). You must be careful not to have overinvested in the client's leaving. Also, you may fail to engage and retain clients if your first recommendation is that the woman terminate her relationship. The client may perceive you as not recognizing the positive characteristics in the relationship and her emotional needs for the relationship. In addition, she may perceive you as judgmental and thinking less of her for experiencing the emotional needs that keep her in the relationship. Because some clients report violence occurring at some point in their relationship and later subsiding, insuring the client's safety does not always mean helping the client leave her partner.

Beyond providing for the client's safety, crisis counseling also serves to help the battered woman realize that you are taking her circumstances seriously. This is particularly important because her defensive style may be to minimize her perceptions of the seriousness and potential dangerousness of her environment. Your intervention can help her examine the specific characteristics of her circumstances while together you strategize safer alternatives. Moreover, because her self-esteem may be so diminished that she is not able to conceptualize functional alternatives, she may need your assistance to begin the process of rebuilding her perceptions of self-worth.

SHORT-TERM COUNSELING

The second goal of therapy is to help the woman identify the impact of the violence on her own emotional functioning. Some clients report symptoms consistent with Post-Traumatic Stress Disorder (PTSD; see Lenore Walker's expanded "Post-Traumatic Stress Reaction and Disorder Interpersonal Violence Diagnostic Criteria," pp. 84-87). These clients are not likely to recognize the basis for their emotional symptoms, and their partners may use these symptoms to further maintain control in the relationship. For example, battered women often report their partners telling them they are emotionally unstable, crazy, or overreacting. Physicians may prescribe medication for the treatment of stress and anxiety, further supporting the client's perception of her own emotional disorder. A diagnosis such as PTSD or Adjustment Disorder may help the client externalize the basis for her symptoms and help her to become an expert on her own reactions to stress. Attributing the symptoms to the battering rather than to the woman's own traits may be most effective with clients who are inclined to request reading material from you. Recognizing the specific precipitant and the predictable pattern of anxiety or depressive reactions can help to increase your client's sense of personal control.

Empowerment is a major goal in working with women who have been battered. Battering is currently conceptualized as a batterer's method of controlling his partner. The client, therefore, has been functioning in a relationship with little personal power or control over her circumstances. Therapy, then, focuses on helping her to regain her sense of personal independence and on helping her shift from focusing on her partner to focusing on her own needs. You can also help the client explore personal resources she may not recognize or may have abandoned at the demand of her partner. Battered women often become increasingly isolated from peers and sources of emotional support. Therefore, you can encourage the client to gradually explore reconnecting with the people she perceives as supportive to her. The client's safety remains paramount in all interventions. You must be cautious when recommending that the client work to change her current environment if these changes are perceived by her as conflicting with the wishes of her partner. If the client does not feel safe in pursuing the specific recommendations, you need to respect her own sense of caution.

LONG-TERM COUNSELING

You can also help the client address the concerns of the past. Clients often feel a need to address their own contributions to the conflict in their relationships. Contributions to conflict can be explored while creating distinctions between verbal conflict, and emotional control and physical abuse. You can help the client recognize that her own feelings of guilt and responsibility for the problems in the relationship are often a function of the abuse of the relationship and not the cause of the abuse, as her partner has maintained.

In the latter stages of therapy you can help the client explore alternatives for the future. Helping the client examine her own resources and acquire new skills increases her sense of power in her own life. Often clients who are battered are emotionally drained and entirely preoccupied with the primary relationship. After the immediate danger is addressed, the client may begin to be ready to expand her perceptions of life's possibilities. Helping the client to open new doors can be an additional source of empowerment for her.

Several cautions are needed in working with women who have been battered. You must examine your own political beliefs and feelings about spouse abuse. Particular sensitivity is required in working with the woman who chooses to stay with an abusive partner. In addition, you need to be careful to speak respectfully of her partner to the client, because clients are emotionally involved with the partner, regardless of the wisdom of that involvement. You need to be sensitive to this emotional attachment and any feelings that may remain. You also need to be sensitive to your own comfort with discussions of the violence. The client may want to speak in graphic detail about her physical or sexual abuse. However, she is only likely to discuss the abuse as long as you are comfortable with the discussion.

Case Example: Catherine. Catherine is a 38-year-old mother of two adolescent daughters. She is in the process of separating from her husband of 20 years. She has come to the therapist at the recommendation of her attorney to help her with parenting skills and to facilitate her positive presentation in court. During the first session, Catherine describes feelings of intense anxiety and fear. She also states she frequently loses her temper at her daughters and is afraid she is a poor parent. Her description of her marriage reveals a pattern of humiliation and manipulation on the part of her husband. Further, she describes her last contact with him at the time of a regularly scheduled visitation with their daughters. He had entered the house to examine some medical insurance forms. They began to argue about responsibility for the deductible. She believes he was trying to renege on his responsibility, using as an excuse that she had not called him before taking her daughter to the emergency room. Catherine states she then asked him to leave but he persisted in arguing. She says she placed her hand on his back to guide him to the door. He flung her arm off and in the process whacked her across the face. The bruise is still visible from the altercation. She states she has been feeling anxious since that time and experiencing panic attacks. She acknowledges having difficulty sleeping and having dreams about prior altercations.

The Therapy. Early on, the therapist inquires about Catherine's future contact with her husband and finds that Catherine has been advised by her attorney to never see her husband without another adult present. The therapist inquires about her husband's treatment of the daughters and is told they protect each other from his psychological manipulation. The therapist, then, interviews Catherine about other possible symptoms and discovers Catherine appears to be suffering from PTSD. She shares this observation with her client and helps normalize the symptoms: "You're not going crazy, this is a very common response to these circumstances. You might expect to feel . . . at times during the coming week." Catherine asks for literature on PTSD and is referred to a support group at a local shelter. Future sessions focus on helping Catherine rebuild her life and reestablish her self-confidence.

ESTABLISHING GOALS IN WORKING WITH BATTERED WOMEN

The following list is offered to assist you in establishing goals for treatment with battered women (Register, 1993):

- *Identification of the Impact of Violence on Functioning.* Clients adjust their entire life to avoid the violence of the spouse. Recognition of the specific alterations and accommodations of behavior are an important component of treatment.

- *Empowerment.* Helping clients shift from a self-perception as victims to individuals who are in charge of their own lives is a slow but important process.

- *Development of Problem-Solving Skills.* Clients need to develop and enhance their skills both in daily living and in interacting with the social agencies that will help improve their circumstances.

- *Interacting With Social Agencies.* Battering brings women into contact with the legal system and many social service agencies. Battered women often become single women and single parents when they separate from their abusive partner. The largest percentage of persons below the poverty level are female single parents, and a majority of women experience a major reduction in income following divorce. Battered women need to learn to obtain the public help that is available to them.

- *Providing Ongoing Support for Battered Women.* Battered women often benefit from support groups that occur concurrently with ongoing psychotherapy.

THERAPY FOR THE BATTERER

Batterers rarely receive treatment voluntarily. They may present in your office seeking help for their spouse. "There's something wrong with my wife, doctor, fix her." Or, you may recognize a batterer during the initial phone request for couples' therapy. An abusive man may focus almost entirely on the negative characteristics of his partner during this initial contact. Or, he may come to treatment with his spouse when one of the children develops problems. In any case, spousal abuse assessment skills will be particularly important for you to develop (see also Table 4, "Checklist of Physical Violence Predispositions," p. 67).

Men who batter are best referred to programs for batterers because therapy for abusive men is most effectively provided by batterers' programs and in group therapy. Reviews of individual treatments suggest that individual counseling is most effective when provided as a supplemental service to group treatment (Gondolf, 1993). Individual sessions with abusive men might also help them to recognize the potential benefits available to them in attending batterer treatment programs. These programs can provide emotional support and help

TABLE 4

Checklist of
Physical Violence Predispositions*

1. Unreasonable jealousy

2. Controlling behavior, initially presented as for the woman's safety and well-being

3. Quick involvement and pressure to make a quick commitment

4 Unrealistic expectations that the partner will meet all of his needs

5. Isolation or cutting the woman off from all resources

6. Blaming others for all his problems

7. Blaming others for his feelings

8. Hypersensitivity: easily insulted or hurt

9. Cruelty to animals and children

10. "Playful" use of force in sex

11. Verbal abuse

12. Rigid sex roles

13. Dr. Jekyll and Mr. Hyde: abrupt mood changes

**14. Past battering

**15. Threats of violence (e.g., "I'll beat the hell out of you")

**16. Breaking or striking objects, especially prized possessions

**17. Use of any force during an argument

---

*Modified with permission from materials developed by the Project for Victims of Family Violence, Inc., Fayetteville, Arkansas.

**These factors are almost always predictive of battering.

batterers acquire alternative strategies for getting their needs met. Moreover, as noted in Chapter 3, not all batterers present with the same psychological profile, and interventions may need to be tailor-made for their needs. For instance, some violent men have drug or alcohol problems and need to receive *simultaneous* treatment for the substance abuse (Cooley, 1993). On the other hand, some batterers have antisocial personalities and are not likely to be responsive to any treatment approach.

The majority of programs for batterers currently recognize a spectrum of violence (Gondolf, 1993; see also Table 5, "Identifying Domestic Violence," pp. 69-70). Such programs address the concern that the threat of violence often continues in homes where physical violence has stopped. Spouse abuse is recognized not as a response to anger but more often as a strategy utilized to maintain power in the relationship. This position of power is regarded as the man's entitlement. He retains this sense of entitlement through self-pity, denial, rationalization, manipulation, and general disregard for his partner. These characteristics are difficult, if not impossible, to challenge in individual therapy. Therefore, skilled group leadership is required for effective treatment.

Current evaluation of treatment programs suggests treatment often requires long-term intervention of 18 months to 2 years. Often the physical violence is reduced, but the verbal threats and control require more intensive intervention (Gondolf, 1993).

The course of therapy with these men (both individually and in group) might also be conceptualized as consisting of three phases which parallel the treatment phases for the battered woman. It is important to consider that the batterer, too, may feel powerless in his interactions with his partner. His feeling of powerlessness expresses itself in greater efforts to control the woman and eventually in greater violence. For him, the major treatment goal will be to help him identify his

TABLE 5

Identifying Domestic Violence*

Domestic Violence may include any of the following:

I. Physical Violence—using one's physical strength or presence to **control** someone

 A. Pushing or shoving

 B. Slapping, grabbing, biting, hitting, spanking, kicking

 C. Holding down, twisting arms, banging head on floor, choking, pinning against wall, carrying against her will

 D. Forced sex

 E. Kneeing, hair pulling, punching

 F. Burning, trying to run over with car

 G. Throwing objects, punching walls or doors, breaking windshields

 H. Breaking or tearing clothes and personal objects

 I. Driving recklessly to scare

 J. Blocking exits or car, taking keys, taking money or bank cards— all to prevent her from leaving

 K. Unplugging the phone

II. Verbal and Emotional Abuse—using one's words or voice to **control** someone

 A. Coercion and threats, including threatening divorce, suicide, reporting her to the authorities, making her do illegal things

 B. Intimidation, including making her afraid by using looks, actions, and gestures

 C. Stalking or checking up on her, accusations of sexual infidelity

---

*Adapted and modified with permission from materials developed by the Domestic Abuse Intervention Project, Duluth, Minnesota.

D. Isolation, including controlling her activities and possessions (e.g., access to the phone, interrogations about her activities, preventing her from seeing friends or family, intense jealousy)

E. Economic abuse including preventing her from working or going to school, controlling the finances

F. Threatening or using the children (e.g., making her feel guilty about the children, threatening to take the children)

G. Invoking male privilege (e.g., treating her like a servant, making all the decisions, defining roles, being master of the castle)

H. Emotional abuse (e.g., putdowns, name calling, denigration, mind games)

---

feelings of vulnerability and learn to channel these in socially appropriate ways (see Table 6, "Batterer Treatment Model Overview," p. 71).

CRISIS INTERVENTION

The crisis intervention phase will include teaching him about violence, the cycle of violence, and the fact that he alone is responsible for the cycle. He also needs to be taught that abuse is often a defense against feelings. Learning to identify the feelings that are defended against is primary. Treatment will then consist of more socially acceptable channeling of these feelings into exercise, sports, or an acknowledgment of vulnerabilities to the partner. The development of a danger-management plan is also key early in treatment. The danger-management plan focuses on teaching the batterer self-control (Segel-Evans, 1991). It involves identifying a list of trigger points, situations, or feelings likely to result in abuse (e.g., "I can't stand it when. . . ."), a list of personal signals that a dangerous situation is developing (e.g., bodily sensations, the appearance of fear in his partner, etc.), a list of steps or techniques to reduce the danger (e.g., time out, positive self-talk, etc.), and a list of steps to reduce the danger over time.

TABLE 6

Batterer Treatment Model Overview

Phase I—Crisis Intervention

A. Educate about violence and violence control

B. Help with the identification of feelings

C. Teach socially acceptable channeling of feelings

D. Develop a danger-management plan

Phase II—Short-Term Counseling

A. Channel power needs into socially acceptable channels

B. Shame and guilt work

C. Explore fears of abandonment

Phase III—Long-Term Counseling

A. Heal abuse of the past

B. Develop relational skills with other men, women, and spouse

SHORT-TERM AND LONG-TERM COUNSELING

Short-term counseling issues involve teaching the batterer ways to rechannel his needs for power into more socially acceptable ways of getting his more basic needs met. Batterers often externalize the blame for the things that happen to them. Unlike other groups who suffer consciously and unreasonably from shame and guilt, batterers are not aware of these feelings, although they may be at the root of violent outbursts.

A goal of short-term counseling may be to examine the existence of these feelings and also those related to fears of abandonment which often also underlie violent outbursts.

Longer term counseling issues may consider healing the abuse of the past (because many batterers were themselves abused) and helping them develop successful relational skills.

Case Example: Mark. Mark, a 39-year-old chef in a successful restaurant, has come in for an intake interview. He seems confused about why he has been referred for counseling, although he does mention that the district attorney told him he must be in counseling for 6 months. Upon further probing, the therapist learns that Mark held his wife Sarah on the bed when she threatened leaving him. Only after considerable additional probing does it become clear that the police were called by Mark and Sarah's neighbors who overhead her screams. They arrived to find Sarah with multiple bruises and lacerations and a broken nose. Mark claims that he only held her down on the bed and does not know how Sarah's injuries occurred. The couple have been married 5 years, Sarah is pregnant with their second child, and they have a history of increasingly more violent arguments. Mark claims this is the first time that things have gotten serious enough for the police to be called. He tells you that Sarah was very sweet when they first met, but that over the last 2 years, she has become increasingly more defiant. She has been wanting to return to work (she is trained as a nurse) but he tells you "No wife of mine will work, as long as I am healthy enough to earn a living." The couple emigrated shortly after their marriage from Israel and have no family or friends in this country.

The Therapy. In working with Mark, the therapist will need to teach him about the cycle of violence and help him accept responsibility for his actions. Learning to identify the feelings which lead to his outbursts and learning how to channel them into more acceptable ways will be paramount. Over the long term, Mark's own family-of-origin issues will need to be explored.

THERAPY WITH THE COUPLE

As long as the man is violent, couples therapy is not recommended. Instead, each member of the couple should be treated separately: the man in a batterers' group with individual therapy adjunctive and the woman in individual therapy with additional support from a group for battered women. Couples therapy should begin only when the violence has stopped and preferably when each member of the couple has received treatment separately.

BEGINNING COUPLES THERAPY: TREATMENT GOALS

Once the violence has ceased, the primary goal of couples therapy is to help the couple establish new patterns of relating. The relationship of couples where violence has existed is usually founded on power and control. The man is afraid of losing his control or is unwilling to share control with his spouse. Your role as therapist is to begin to modify patterns of communication that serve to maintain the negative qualities of the relationship. Both partners must begin to recognize the benefit in mutual sharing of power and must acknowledge that in any relationship no one wins if one person loses.

A positive focus of treatment can be to help the couple reconnect with the qualities in each other that were the initial foundation of the relationship. Most couples can begin to identify the positive qualities that attracted them to each other. In addition, most couples can recall times when they enjoyed each other and did not fight. The oft-quoted saying "The opposite of love is not hate but indifference" is often true for couples who choose to stay together after the violence has stopped. Helping the couple identify the love in the relationship provides the therapist with the flexibility to explore more difficult topics.

Many batterers have emotional vulnerabilities in addition to the proclivity for violence. These vulnerabilities are often hidden by the violent behavior and the need to control the relationship through manipulation or violence. Couples therapy may provide the opportunity to explore these vulnerabilities with the partner in the presence of a safe outsider. You need to protect both members of the couple as these vulnerabilities and hidden concerns are explored. The battered woman is likely to continue to feel anger toward her spouse and may feel a desire to direct this anger toward him as he exposes this softer side of himself. The batterer is likely to have difficulty acknowledging these concerns and may minimize or be quick to terminate the exploration. You are responsible for monitoring the process and insuring the safety of both clients during the sessions and after they leave your office.

LATER THERAPY: TREATMENT GOALS

You are also responsible for helping clients acquire new skills of conflict resolution. Differences of opinion are present in all relationships. Few couples are skilled at mutually discussing and resolving their differences. You can help the couple explore new strategies and maintain the level of emotional intensity so as to allow good work to take place. Conflict resolution may be approached later in the course of therapy after trust has had an opportunity to be reestablished in the relationship.

Several cautions are needed for therapists who are working with couples where violence has occurred. First, as with any therapy, the safety of the clients is paramount. If at any time you believe that your own safety or the safety of either client cannot be insured, therapy should be terminated and other safety precautions undertaken. Second, it is critical that you be perceived as mutually supportive and not aligned with either member of the couple. The purpose of couples therapy is to help develop a mutually supportive relationship that benefits both members. It is also possible that, through the course of therapy, one or the other partner may begin to recognize they are no longer invested in the relationship and decide they would like to separate from their partner. At this point, the direction of therapy would change and the focus might be toward a safe dissolution of the relationship. Third, you must be aware of your own political beliefs and refrain from allowing these beliefs to influence the course of treatment. When the therapist approaches the couple with caution and sensitivity, therapy can help couples who wish to stay together develop more functional and supportive relationships.

Case Example: Joe and Bonnie. Joe and Bonnie have come to therapy for help with their marriage. Joe has called the therapist and reports his wife has become extensively involved in the Parent/Teachers Association (PTA). As a consequence, he is afraid the family is suffering. The therapist agrees to see the couple. Both partners come to the initial session. Bonnie admits that, now that the children are in school, she has become very active in the PTA. However, when Joe first indicated he felt this was having an impact on the family, she agreed to reduce her involvement and consider counseling. Joe and Bonnie have been married for 15 years. They have three children, ages 10, 11, and 13. The children reportedly do well in school and are involved in local sporting activities. Bonnie indicates that she has been very involved in the children's school and extracurricular activities during the past 3 years. Prior to that time, she stayed at home. Joe indicates Bonnie has not worked since their marriage. "I think a mother should be home with the children," he states. The couple describes positive experiences prior to the birth of the children. Activities revolved around Joe's friends and the many parties and afternoon cookouts the couple attended. Bonnie reports Joe began to drink more at these parties after their first child was born. Joe retorts that everyone drank. Bonnie indicates that she started to stay home with the children rather than go to the parties and states that Joe would often be driven home by his friends because he was too drunk to drive. She also indicates that when she complained about the drinking he lashed out and pushed her away. She admits she was afraid of her husband and feels angry that she was made to feel afraid. Both members of the couple agree drinking is no longer a problem. Joe stopped drinking when he received a DUI 3 years ago and lost his license for 6 months. Both members of the couple agree they don't feel as close to each other as they did when they were first married. They are particularly concerned with the impact of their differences on the children. Their daughter has been reluctant to leave home to go to school and they are afraid their conflict might be partially responsible. They both agree that violence in the relationship has stopped. Bonnie acknowledges residual anger but is not currently afraid of her husband.

The Therapy. With this couple, the initial phase of therapy focuses on helping the clients rediscover the joy and pleasure they felt with each other early in the marriage. Therapy also explores what they perceive as the characteristics of a positive mature marriage and how they envision themselves in that role. In therapy, Joe and Bonnie begin to explore characteristics of the earlier relationship, especially those that could be characterized as less mature and more fear-based. The therapist normalizes these fears and places them in an appropriate developmental context. After this positive foundation is established, the couple explores specific areas of conflict in their relationship. The therapist highlights the benefit to both partners of mutual support for individual growth within the relationship.

THERAPY WITH CHILDREN

Children are most often brought to therapy by one or both parents. Many children themselves have experienced physical abuse and require treatment for their own experience of trauma. Other children have witnessed the physical violence in the couple. Children's responses to spouse abuse frequently range from aggression to withdrawal to somatic complaints (Hughes, Parkinson, & Vargo, 1989). The specific symptoms dictate the recommended intervention.

As with all treatment approaches, the immediate safety to the client is paramount. Safety is determined by the current presence of violence, specifically whether the batterer has stopped battering. This is important to assess in relation to children of violent families, because both witnessing abuse and experiencing it are recognized as traumatic (Hughes et al., 1989). Currently, most divorced men who have abused their wives are allowed to continue to visit their children (Liss & Stahly, 1993; Stahly, 1993). Children who have not recovered from the trauma may reexperience feelings of trauma when they are in the presence of the abusive parent. Scheduled visits with the batterer can lead to a continued experience of trauma for the children. Thus, your first responsibility is to examine the quantity and quality of contact with the abusive parent in order to determine the extent of ongoing trauma to the children.

THE CHILDREN'S NEEDS

Children may need the experience of "symbolic" safety. The child may continue to experience intense fear and fearful symptoms such as nightmares even when the abuse has stopped or the abusive parent has left the home. Frequent reassurance and symbols of protection against the abuser will help the child address the symptoms of trauma. For example, one strategy used by a therapist was to recommend that a child read about aggressive guard dogs and imagine the most protective, ferocious beast possible, immediately before going to sleep. The dog, then, could protect the child from the batterer in the child's dreams.

Children who were emotionally neglected while the family's energy focused on surviving the violence may need limits set on behavior they acquired while no one was looking. Such children, who have experienced little structure, may be resistant to rules applied by the now attentive parent. In addition, parents may experience a sense of guilt for not creating the perfect home environment. This guilt is likely to interfere with effective discipline. Parents, too, may be too emotionally exhausted by the violence to provide consistency in the home. Learning to implement structure within the home is often a first step in rebuilding a family after the violence has stopped (Hansen, 1993).

Children may experience ambivalent feelings toward the abusive parent. These feelings may be particularly persistent if the children continue to have contact with the parent who is *no longer* violent. Children may feel some genuine liking for their father but also some guilt for liking a person who has been so harmful toward their mother. Helping children express this love while also expressing their anger at their father's behavior aids them in resolving this sense of disloyalty and confusion. In addition, fathers who have stopped the violence may maintain the same manipulative style and attempt to control their spouse through their influence with the children. The children, therefore, may perceive that they can gain favor with their father by challenging their mother. This pattern is particularly challenging for the therapist, who is often addressing the father's abusive style in absentia. One approach is to help the mother to require respect from her child while allowing the child to experience the ambivalent feelings toward the father. Children are far more likely to respect mothers who respect themselves, and the mother's own empowerment therapy will help in her relationships with her children. The process of therapy for the child, therefore, involves all members of the family.

THE CHILDREN'S BEHAVIOR

Children who have witnessed abusive fathers are more likely to abuse their mothers than children who have not (Carlson, 1990). As discussed earlier, you must address the issue of safety for the parents. Abusive children are to be regarded as dangerous and appropriate agencies should be involved in treatment. Mothers who have been battered may be less likely to identify their children's actions as requiring outside intervention. You will need to help the family accept the appropriate interventions, including hospitalization, or foster care if needed.

Alternatively, children who have witnessed abuse may become particularly protective of their parents. Individual sessions with these children may reveal a desire to return to age-appropriate interests. Most effective interventions may involve intense treatment of the parents with peripheral and occasional brief conjoint sessions with the children. These children may feel a sense of relief that an adult has taken on the role of protector and emotional supporter, thereby allowing them to return to the role of child.

Women who are battered may believe compliance and respect is achieved through instilling fear in their children. These children are likely to be engaging in a replication of the power struggle that existed between their parents. Such families need to acquire new skills and new experiences of respect for each other. These children need to acquire the desire for their parents' approval and respect for their mothers through the therapeutic process.

Some children may themselves be experiencing the symptoms of Post-Traumatic Stress Disorder. Such symptoms as sleep disturbance, appetite disturbance, poor concentration (particularly in school), increased irritability, and angry outbursts may suggest symptoms of major trauma. Such children may need individual therapy and an opportunity to correct the emotional experience. However, mothers often request individual treatment for their children; you need to be extremely careful that the family's needs for intervention are addressed as well. As noted, many such children experience problems respecting their parents or really want the therapist to help them return to a "normal" life. Often time spent with the parent may best take the form of a relaxed afternoon at the playground.

CAUTIONS IN WORKING WITH CHILDREN

In working with children from abusive families, your role as therapist is first to insure the safety of the children from potential child abuse by the batterer, from emotional manipulation by the batterer, or from frustrated physical violence from their mother. Some children, particularly males, are perceived by their mothers to resemble the abuser and, therefore, may be the recipient of displaced anger. You will need to identify how the individual child has coped with the violence and recognize that some coping strategies, such as denial, might be adaptive. You will also need to attend to the request of the parents regarding the treatment provided for the child and respect the requests. However, caution is recommended in allowing any parent to "dictate" treatment. For example, throughout the course of treatment, you may need to interact with the abusive parent, who may not have the best interests of the children in mind, while providing therapy to the children.

The aforementioned considerations address treatment issues of children when the violence in the marriage has stopped or the marriage has terminated. Treatment considerations for children in families where battering is continuing are similar. It is imperative that you, the therapist, conduct an accurate assessment of the violence. First, is the child in danger and does a report of child abuse need to be filed? Second, how often is the child witnessing the abuse and how extreme is the abuse involved? Third, how is the child perceiving the abuse, that is, does the child feel protective toward the abused or the abuser? Fourth, what strategies does the child employ to cope with the violence? For example, such children often will leave the home and seek support with a neighbor. Strategies that insure the safety of the child should be encouraged, especially until you, the therapist, can help to stop the couple's violence. We recommend that parents be included and informed of most interventions. An exception is made to insure the safety of the child from the abusive parent. For example, both parents might be told of the child's fears but not of the child's hiding place where the child goes to avoid the abusive parent. Any symptoms the child is experiencing are not likely to respond to treatment until the trauma of the battering in the home stops. Treatment will be crisis oriented and focused primarily on strategies for the emotional safety of the child until the violence in the marriage is addressed and stops. Because 30% to 60% of all batterers batter their children as well (Hughes, 1982; Straus, 1980), whenever the child's physical safety is in danger, protective services must be contacted and the case treated as with any case of child endangerment.

Case Example: Bill. Bill is a 14-year-old living with his mother and sister, Amy, age 10. Bill's mother indicates that she divorced the children's father 2 years ago, after a tumultuous marriage. The children visit their father every other weekend. Amy often becomes ill before the visits and as a result visits him infrequently. Both children acknowledge their father was violent toward their mother. At one time the mother was hospitalized with broken ribs and the family stayed at a shelter for 2 weeks. After this most violent episode, divorce proceedings were begun.

Bill is currently challenging his mother and requesting increased independence. His curfew is 10:00 p.m. on weekends and he wants this extended to "at least 11:00 p.m." He does well in school and is involved in sports. His mother is concerned with his "attitude around the house." She complains that his room is a mess and she has to remind him constantly to complete his chores. She acknowledges she is also concerned with her daughter's clear desire not to visit her father. Bill indicates he has other things he would rather do on weekends, as well, but admits that sometimes his father takes him to sporting events which he enjoys.

The Therapy. After a thorough evaluation, family therapy is initiated. Much of Bill's behavior is normalized as age-appropriate adolescent behavior. Therapy focuses on helping the family develop skills for conflict resolution and compromise. Bill offers to try to help his sister cope with the visits with their father. Positive characteristics of the family are highlighted, particularly Bill's traits that are resourceful and different from his father's. Therapy helps the family unite to formulate creative strategies for containing the weekend visits with the father. The children's feelings of ambivalence and the mother's struggle with these feelings are shared openly among the family members. Therapy is relatively short term and terminated with the understanding that further consultation is available if needed.

SUMMARY

The first goal of treatment, with the battered woman, the batterer, the couple, and the children, is to insure the safety of the clients. The battering must stop or the clients must leave the battering situation before treatment of the trauma that results from battering can begin. All treatments, therefore, begin with crisis intervention, attention to immediate needs for safety, and problem solving of immediate concerns. The second component of all treatment is to help the client(s) regain the resources and self-worth that preceded the trauma of the abuse. These resources are needed for the healing process. The battered woman needs to become again the person she once was prior to the loss of self-esteem she experienced as a victim of abuse. The batterer needs to access the resources to control his behavior. The couple, if they are to remain a couple, need to access the positive characteristics and experiences that brought them together and that they have shared throughout their relationship. The children need to explore their own strengths and coping strategies to help them recover from the trauma and fully develop as individuals. Lastly, all clients need to learn to function beyond the battering and discover themselves, their strengths, and their limitations, following the treatment for the trauma of abuse.

Post-Traumatic Stress Reaction and Disorder Interpersonal Violence Diagnostic Criteria*

1. Experiencing a traumatic abusive and violent event **(caused by one or more individuals)** that is outside of the range of usual human experience **(such as sexual abuse and exploitation, assault and battery, gender and racial discrimination, hate crimes)** that would be markedly distressing to almost anyone. **The traumatic event may be experienced one time or over a repeated period.****

2. **Changes in cognition or in the way people think about the world and themselves.** The traumatic event is persistently reexperienced in at least *three* of the following ways:

   a. recurrent and intrusive distressing recollections of the event **(spontaneous and ruminations)**

   b. recurrent distressing dreams of the event

---

*Modified by Lenore Walker, EdD, from the *DSM-III-R*. **Boldface indicates her new criteria.** The *(DSM-IV)* criteria for PTSD (309.81) are not substantially different from the *DSM-III-R* criteria (309.89) used by Walker in applying PTSD symptoms to survivors of interpersonal violence.

**Measure whether trauma reaches threshold level by clinical judgment after evaluating the individual's abuse history or by using the Severity of Psychosocial Stressor Scale, as follows:*

Level 4: Severe

Single event—rape, life-threatening assault, enduring circumstances (ongoing physical and sexual abuse, sexual exploitation, serious psychological harassment)

Level 5: Extreme

Being held hostage, kidnapped, near-death experiences

Level 6: Catastrophic

Ritual abuse

    c. sudden acting or feeling as if the traumatic event were recurring (includes a sense of reliving the experience, illusions, hallucinations, and dissociative and/or flashback episodes, even those that occur upon awakening or when intoxicated)

    d. intense psychological distress at exposure to events that symbolize or resemble an aspect of the traumatic event, including anniversaries of the trauma

    e. **interference with normal learning activities because of bad memories, attention deficits, difficulty in concentrating, or relating to teachers or supervisors**

    f. **increased ability to intensely focus on areas other than those which cause distress or pain. In extreme cases, dissociation or fragmented and multiple personalities occur.**

    g. **obsessive thoughts about the abuser(s)**

    h. **confused thinking**

3. **Changes in affect demonstrated by depression-like symptoms.** Persistent avoidance of stimuli associated with the trauma or numbing of general responsiveness (not present before the trauma) as indicated by at least *four* of the following:

    a. efforts to avoid thoughts or feelings associated with the trauma

    b. efforts to avoid activities or situations that arouse recollection of the trauma

    c. inability to recall an important aspect of the trauma (psychogenic amnesia, denial, minimization, and repression in repeated trauma)

    d. marked diminished interest in significant activities

    e. **intense periods of sadness with or without crying**

    f. restricted range of affect **(including fear of own anger)**

    g. sense of a foreshortened future or death

    h. **self-mutilation and/or suicidal ideation and attempts**

    i. **use of alcohol or drugs to avoid feelings**

4. Persistent symptoms of increased arousal **and anxiety symptoms** as indicated by at least *four* of the following:

a. difficulty falling or staying asleep

b. **difficulty in eating properly**

c. irritability or outbursts of anger

d. difficulty concentrating and attention disorders

e. hypervigilance to cues of potential danger

f. exaggerated startle response

g. physiologic reactivity upon exposure to events that symbolize or resemble an aspect of the traumatic event **(somatization, psychophysiological disorders, anxiety disorders, immunological deficits, and other high stress symptoms)**

h. **anxiety or panic attacks**

i. **increased fearfulness and phobic reactions**

j. **temporary increase in activity level**

5. Changes in interpersonal relationships. **Different types of changes in relationships occur when trauma was experienced in the family, by a person in a trusted position of authority, included sexual components, and occurred more than one time. Indicated by presence of at least *three* of the following:**

   a. **feelings of detachment or estrangement from others (feel different, lack of trust, fear of betrayal)**

   b. **isolation from friends and family**

   c. **inability to be alone (or separate from abuser)**

   d. **confusion between emotional and sexual intimacy**

   e. **sexual dysfunction (lack of sexual desire, inappropriate sexual conduct, fear of sex, sexual acting out)**

   f. **increased need for power and control over individuals less powerful than themselves (both overt and covert manipulation)**

   g. **difficulty in respecting boundaries and limits between themselves and other people**

   h. **extreme compliance and need to please others**

6. Duration of less than 6 weeks gets coded as a Post-Traumatic Stress Reaction (PTSR) and more than 6 weeks is coded as a Post-Traumatic Stress Disorder (PTSD).

5

A Final Word on
Spouse Abuse

This book explores current approaches to the assessment
and treatment of spouse abuse. Chapter 1 mentions that
spouse abuse occurs in 20% to 50% of the population. Thirty
percent to 60% of batterers also abuse their children (Hughes,
1982; Straus, 1980). Clinicians who do not specialize in the
treatment of battering have indicated that as much as 60% of
their client caseload may have experienced domestic violence.
Battering occurs in couples from all ethnic and socioeconomic
backgrounds, and alcohol abuse may intensify the likelihood
of battering (from 48% to 87% of alcohol abusers are batterers
[Cooley, 1993]).

As our self-quiz (Chapter 2) suggests, numerous myths
exist about spousal abuse. These myths include:

- definitions of domestic violence (the close relationship
  between psychological abuse and physical abuse and
  how spousal abuse manifests)

- the prevalence and seriousness of spousal abuse (much
  more prevalent and serious than most believe)

- the kind of woman who is battered (any woman) and
  her responsibility for the violence (the responsibility
  is always that of the batterer)

- the dynamics of battering (the batterer may have a history of abuse of various kinds but he is likely to be like most men in his personality profile)

- treatment and assessment issues (the need for safety planning and the importance of assessment)

- legal and ethical issues (laws covering therapists and protection provided by the authorities)

In Chapter 3, we emphasized that assessment of spouse abuse requires careful screening of all clients who request therapy. Clients who request treatment from practitioners rarely present spouse abuse as their primary reason for seeking services. Victims of abuse may present with symptoms of depression or anxiety, batterers may seek help for their wives, and children who have witnessed abuse may present with behavioral problems. However, we maintain that battering occurs so frequently that all clients should be assessed for a history of experiencing, committing, or witnessing battering.

The most critical concern in any assessment is the determination of the immediate danger to the client or members of the client's family. The familiar questions of who, what, when, where, and how serve as guidelines in evaluating the frequency and severity of the violence. The therapist should err on the side of thoroughness in conducting the evaluation. Therapists must recognize that many victims of abuse do not return for a second visit; thus, the first visit is the only opportunity to insure the safety of the client. Work with the couple, the batterer, or the children in families where abuse occurs requires the same thoroughness and the same approach to insuring safety.

The second component of assessment requires an evaluation of the functioning of the client. What should be examined are the practical and emotional resources available to the client. This should be examined in the case of the battered woman, the batterer, the couple, and the children of the abuse. Assessment of functioning includes cognitive, emotional, and practical factors because these resources will be called upon throughout the intervention.

The therapist must acknowledge that spouse abuse is not socially desirable. Therefore, social expectations may interfere with a client's willingness to disclose violence. Consequently, interviews need to occur individually with each family member to insure that presence of others in the family does not restrict the amount of self-disclosure. This approach is required when working with all members of the family: with the battered woman, the batterer, and the children. Children may be especially reluctant to disclose the violence in the presence of their parents for fear of appearing disloyal to one of the parents.

In Chapter 4, we detailed treatment issues. Crisis intervention begins during the first stage of treatment and may occur throughout therapy. Safety from abuse and stopping the violence are the two primary considerations. Therapists may need to reconceptualize their traditional role to include helping clients contact social and legal agencies. Batterers may need concurrent treatment at drug and alcohol facilities and batterers' groups. Battered women will also need help interacting with social agencies, because often a consequence of long-term abuse is inability to deal with practical life situations. Therapists may be required to facilitate the coordination and integration of these services.

Treatment for battering requires long-term intervention. The recovery of battered women and the batterers' acceptance of responsibility for the violence may be a slow process even among motivated clients. Many women return to abusive spouses several times before leaving, and the prognosis for batterers (especially without treatment) is poor. Children too, may require treatment. Therapists need to be careful not to become discouraged, to be pleased with small steps toward growth, and not to expect rapid change. Recovery can occur, but may require many different visits to many different therapists. Certainly with appropriate treatment, new families can be created once the abuse is no longer present—new families formed with hope and respect.

References

American Psychiatric Association. (1987). *Diagnostic and Statistical Manual of Mental Disorders* (3rd ed. rev.). Washington, DC: Author.

American Psychiatric Association. (1994). *Diagnostic and Statistical Manual of Mental Disorders* (4th ed.). Washington, DC: Author.

Berman, P. (1993). Impact of marital abuse relationships on children. In M. Hansen & M. Harway (Eds.), *Battering and Family Therapy: A Feminist Perspective* (pp. 134-146). Newbury Park, CA: Sage.

Bodin, A. M. (1992). *Relationship Conflict Inventory*. Mimeographed instrument. (For additional information, contact Arthur M. Bodin, PhD, 555 Middlefield Road, Palo Alto, CA 94301-2141 or telephone 415-328-3000.)

Brown, S. L. (1991). *Counseling Victims of Violence*. Alexandria, VA: American Association for Counseling and Development.

Browne, A. (1987). *When Battered Women Kill*. New York: Free Press.

Burgess, A. W., Hartman, C. R., & Kelly, S. J. (1990). Assessing child abuse: The triads checklist. *Journal of Psychosocial Nursing, 28,* 7-14.

Carlson, B. E. (1990). Adolescent observers of marital violence. *Journal of Family Violence, 5,* 285-299.

Cervantes, N. N. (1993). Therapist duty in domestic violence cases: Ethical considerations. In M. Hansen & M. Harway (Eds.), *Battering and Family Therapy: A Feminist Perspective* (pp. 147-155). Newbury Park, CA: Sage.

Cheney, A. B., & Bleker, E. G. (1982, August). *Internal-External Locus of Control and Repression-Sensitization in Battered Women.* Paper presented at the annual meeting of the American Psychological Association, Washington, DC.

Connors, J., & Harway, M. (1994). *Commonalities Among Forms of Abuse and Male-Female Power Relationships.* Article submitted for publication.

Cooley, C. S. (1993). Establishing feminist systemic criteria for viewing violence and alcoholism. In M. Hansen & M. Harway (Eds.), *Battering and Family Therapy: A Feminist Perspective* (pp. 217-226). Newbury Park, CA: Sage.

Cummings, J. S., Pellegrini, D. S., Notarius, C. I., & Cummings, E. M. (1989). Children's responses to angry adult behavior as a function of marital distress and history of interparent hostility. *Child Development, 60,* 1035-1043.

Davidson, T. (1978). *Conjugal Crime: Understanding and Changing the Wife Beating Pattern.* New York: Hawthorne.

Dobash, R. E., & Dobash, R. P. (1977-1978). Wives: The "appropriate" victims of marital violence. *Victimology, 2,* 426-442.

Dobash, R. E., & Dobash, R. P. (1979). *Violence Against Wives: A Case Against the Patriarchy.* New York: Free Press.

Edleson, J. L., Eisikovits, Z. C., & Guttman, E. (1985). Men who batter women: A critical review of the evidence. *Journal of Family Issues, 6,* 229-247.

Feldman, S. E. (1983). Battered women: Psychological correlates of the victimization process. *Dissertation Abstracts International, 44,* 1221-B.

Ferraro, K. J., & Johnson, J. M. (1983). How women experience battering: The process of victimization. *Social Problems, 30,* 325-339.

Follingstad, D. R., Neckerman, A. P., & Vormbrock, J. (1988). Reactions to victimization and coping strategies of battered women: The ties that bind. *Clinical Psychology Review, 8,* 373-390.

Gaquin, D. A. (1977-1978). Spouse abuse: Data from the National Crime Survey. *Victimology, 2,* 632-642.

Gelles, R. J., & Strauss, M. R. (1989). *Intimate Violence: The Causes and Consequences of Abuse in the American Family.* New York: Simon & Schuster.

Giles-Sims, J. (1983). *Wife Battering: A Systems Theory Approach.* New York: Guilford.

Gondolf, E. (1993). Treating the batterer. In M. Hansen & M. Harway (Eds.), *Battering and Family Therapy: A Feminist Perspective* (pp. 105-118). Newbury Park, CA: Sage.

Goodstein, R. K., & Page, A. W. (1981). Battered wife syndrome: Overview of dynamics and treatment. *American Journal of Psychiatry, 138,* 1036-1044.

Hanks, S. E., & Rosenbaum, C. P. (1977). Battered women: A study of women who live with violent alcohol-abusing men. *American Journal of Orthopsychiatry, 47,* 291-306.

Hansen, M. (1993). *When Battering Ends in Divorce: Interventions with Family Members--The Children.* Symposium presented at the annual midwinter conference of Division of Family Psychology, San Diego, CA.

Hansen, M., & Harway, M. (1993). Directions for future generations of therapists. In M. Hansen & M. Harway (Eds.), *Battering and Family Therapy: A Feminist Perspective* (pp. 227-251). Newbury Park, CA: Sage.

Hansen, M., Harway, M., & Cervantes, N. N. (1991). Therapists' perceptions of severity in cases of family violence. *Violence and Victims, 4,* 275-286.

Hart, B. J. (1993). The legal road to freedom. In M. Hansen & M. Harway (Eds.), *Battering and Family Therapy: A Feminist Perspective* (pp. 13-29). Newbury Park, CA: Sage.

Harway, M., & Hansen, M. (1990). Therapists' recognition of wife battering: Some empirical evidence. *Family Violence Bulletin, 6,* 16-18.

Harway, M., & Hansen, M. (1993a). An overview of domestic violence. In M. Hansen & M. Harway (Eds.), *Battering and Family Therapy: A Feminist Perspective* (pp. 1-12). Newbury Park, CA: Sage.

Harway, M., & Hansen, M. (1993b). Therapist perceptions of family violence. In M. Hansen & M. Harway (Eds.), *Battering and Family Therapy: A Feminist Perspective* (pp. 42-53). Newbury Park, CA: Sage.

Hendricks-Matthews, M. (1982). The battered woman: Is she ready for help? *Social Casework, 63,* 131-137.

Holtzworth-Munroe, A., Waltz, J., Jacobson, N. S., Monaco, V., Fehrenbach, P. A., & Gottman, J. M. (1992). Recruiting nonviolent men as control subjects for research on marital violence: How easily can it be done? *Violence and Victims, 7,* 79-88.

Hotaling, G. T., & Sugarman, D. B. (1986). An analysis of risk markers in husband to wife violence: The current state of knowledge. *Violence and Victims, 1,* 101-124.

Hudson, W. W., & McIntosh, S. R. (1981, November). The assessment of spouse abuse: Two quantifiable dimensions. *Journal of Marriage and the Family, 43,* 873-888.

Hughes, H. M. (1982). Brief interventions with children in a battered women's shelter: A model preventive program. *Family Relations, 31,* 495-502.

Hughes, H. M., Parkinson, D., & Vargo, M. (1989). Witnessing spouse abuse and experiencing physical abuse: A double whammy? *Journal of Family Violence, 4,* 197-209.

Jaffe, P. G., Wolfe, D. A., & Wilson, S. K. (1990). *Children of Battered Women: Issues in Child Development and Intervention Planning.* Newbury Park, CA: Sage.

Koss, M. P. (1990). The women's mental health agenda: Violence against women. *American Psychologist, 45,* 374-380.

Lisak, D., & Roth, S. (1988). Motivational factors in nonincarcerated sexually aggressive men. *Journal of Personality and Social Psychology, 55,* 795-802.

Liss, M. B., & Stahly, G. B. (1993). Domestic violence and child custody. In M. Hansen & M. Harway (Eds.), *Battering and Family Therapy: A Feminist Perspective* (pp. 175-187). Newbury Park, CA: Sage.

Miller, E. T., & Porter, C. A. (1983). Self-blame in victims of violence. *Journal of Social Issues, 39,* 139-152.

Okun, L. (1986). *Woman Abuse: Facts Replacing Myths.* Albany, NY: State University of New York Press.

O'Neil, J. M., & Egan, J. (1993). Abuses of power against women: Sexism, gender role conflict, psychological violence. In E. Cook (Ed.), *Women, Relationships and Power: Implications for Counseling* (pp. 49-78). Alexandria, VA: ACA Press.

Pagelow, M. D. (1989). *The Forgotten Victims: Children of Domestic Violence.* Paper prepared for presentation at the Domestic Violence Seminar of the Los Angeles County Domestic Violence Council.

Pillemer, K. A., & Suitor, J. J. (1991). Sharing a residence with an adult child: A cause of psychological distress in the elderly? *American Journal of Orthopsychiatry, 61,* 144-148.

Price, D., & Hansen, M. (1991). *Murder/Suicide in Families: Warning Sign for Therapists.* Paper presented at the annual convention of the American Psychological Association, San Francisco, CA.

Pryor, J. (1992). *The Social Psychology of Sexual Harassment: Person and Situation Factors Which Give Rise to Sexual Harassment.* Paper presented at the National Conference on Sex and Power Issues in the Workplace, Washington, DC.

Ramsey-Klawsnik, H. (1993). Interviewing elders for suspected elder abuse: Guidelines and techniques. *Journal of Elder Abuse and Neglect, 5,* 73-90.

Register, E. (1993). Feminism and recovering: Working with the individual woman. In M. Hansen & M. Harway (Eds.), *Battering and Family Therapy: A Feminist Perspective* (pp. 93-104). Newbury Park, CA: Sage.

Renzetti, C. M. (1993). Violence in lesbian relationships. In M. Hansen & M. Harway (Eds.), *Battering and Family Therapy: A Feminist Perspective* (pp. 188-199). Newbury Park, CA: Sage.

Segel-Evans, K. (1991). *Safety Self-Control Planning.* Unpublished manuscript.

Segel-Evans, K. (1994). *Treatment Issues for Men Who Batter.* Paper presented at the Midwinter Convention of Divisions 29, 42, and 43 of the American Psychological Association, Scottsdale, AZ.

Stahly, G. B. (1993). *When Battering Ends in Divorce: Interventions with Family Members--Custody Issues.* Symposium presented at the annual midwinter convention of APA Division of Family Psychology, San Diego, CA.

Steinmetz, S. (1977). Wife-beating, husband-beating: A comparison of the use of physical violence between spouses to resolve marital fights. In M. Roy (Ed.), *Battered Women: A Psychosocial Study of Domestic Violence* (pp. 63-67). New York: Van Nostrand Reinhold.

Straus, M. A. (1980). The marriage license as hitting license: Evidence from popular culture, law, and social science. In M. A. Straus & G. T. Hotaling (Eds.), *The Social Causes of Husband/Wife Violence* (pp. 39-50). Minneapolis: University Park Press.

Straus, M. A., & Gelles, R. J. (1988). How violent are American families? Estimates from the National Family Violence Resurvey and other studies. In G. T. Hotaling, D. Finkelhor, J. T. Kirkpatrick, & M. A. Straus (Eds.), *Family Abuse and Its Consequences: New Directions in Research* (pp. 14-36). Newbury Park, CA: Sage.

Straus, M. A., Gelles, R. J., & Steinmetz, S. K. (1980). *Behind Closed Doors: Violence in the American Family.* Garden City, NY: Anchor/Doubleday.

Walker, L. E. A. (1979). *The Battered Woman.* New York: Harper & Row.

Walker, L. E. A. (1984). *The Battered Woman Syndrome.* New York: Springer.

Warshaw, C. (1989, December). Limitations of the medical model in the care of battered women. *Gender and Society, 3,* 506-517.

U.S. Commission on Civil Rights. (1982). *Under the Rule of Thumb: Battered Women and the Administration of Justice.* Washington, DC: U.S. Government Printing Office.

Index

If You Found This Book Useful . . .

You might want to know more about our other titles.

If you would like to receive our latest catalog, please return this form:

Name:_____
(Please Print)

Address:_____

Address:_____

City/State/Zip:_____

Telephone:(_____)_____

I am a:

_____ Psychologist   _____ Mental Health Counselor
_____ Psychiatrist   _____ Marriage and Family Therapist
_____ School Psychologist   _____ Not in Mental Health Field
_____ Clinical Social Worker   _____ Other:_____

◆   ◆   ◆

Professional Resource Press
P.O. Box 15560
Sarasota, FL 34277-1560

Telephone #813-366-7913
FAX #813-366-7971

Add A Colleague To Our Mailing List . . .

If you would like us to send our latest catalog to one of your colleagues, please return this form.

Name:_____
(Please Print)

Address:_____

Address:_____

City/State/Zip:_____

Telephone:(_____)_____

I am a:

_____ Psychologist   _____ Mental Health Counselor
_____ Psychiatrist   _____ Marriage and Family Therapist
_____ School Psychologist   _____ Not in Mental Health Field
_____ Clinical Social Worker   _____ Other:_____

◆   ◆   ◆

Professional Resource Press
P.O. Box 15560
Sarasota, FL 34277-1560

Telephone #813-366-7913
FAX #813-366-7971

Add A Colleague To Our Mailing List . . .

If you would like us to send our latest catalog to one of your colleagues, please return this form.

Name:_____
(Please Print)

Address:_____

Address:_____

City/State/Zip:_____

Telephone:(_____)_____

I am a:

_____	Psychologist	_____	Mental Health Counselor
_____	Psychiatrist	_____	Marriage and Family Therapist
_____	School Psychologist	_____	Not in Mental Health Field
_____	Clinical Social Worker	_____	Other:_____

◆   ◆   ◆

Professional Resource Press
P.O. Box 15560
Sarasota, FL 34277-1560

Telephone #813-366-7913
FAX #813-366-7971

If You Found This Book Useful . . .

You might want to know more about our other titles.

If you would like to receive our latest catalog, please return this form:

Name:_____
(Please Print)

Address:_____

Address:_____

City/State/Zip:_____

Telephone:(_____)_____

I am a:

_____ Psychologist		_____ Mental Health Counselor	
_____ Psychiatrist		_____ Marriage and Family Therapist	
_____ School Psychologist		_____ Not in Mental Health Field	
_____ Clinical Social Worker		_____ Other:_____	

◆   ◆   ◆

Professional Resource Press
P.O. Box 15560
Sarasota, FL 34277-1560

Telephone #813-366-7913
FAX #813-366-7971